Meditation
&
Reality
A CRITICAL VIEW

Douglas A. Fox

Unless otherwise indicated, Scripture quotations are from the Revised Standard Version of the Holy Bible, copyright, 1946, 1952, and © 1971, 1973 by the Division of Christian Education, National Council of the Churches of Christ in the U.S.A., and used by permission.

Acknowledgment is made for permission to quote from the following sources:

To Brown University for Norman Melchert, "Mystical Experience and Ontological Claims," *Philosophy and Phenomenological Research* 37 (June 1977): 445–463.

To the Hutchinson Publishing Group Limited for Lama Anagarika Govinda, *Foundations of Tibetan Mysticism* (New York: E. P. Dutton, 1960). Reprinted with the permission of the Hutchinson Publishing Group Limited.

To New Directions for Thomas Merton: NEW SEEDS OF CONTEMPLATION. Copyright © 1961 by The Abbey of Gethsemani, Inc. Reprinted by permission of New Directions Publishing Corporation.

To Charles Scribner's Sons for Martin Buber, excerpted from *I and Thou*. Translation copyright © 1970 Charles Scribner's Sons. Reprinted with the permission of Charles Scribner's Sons.

To Sheed and Ward Limited for Saint Teresa, *The Complete Works of St. Teresa of Jesus*, translated by E. Allison Peers (London: Sheed and Ward Limited, 1946). Reprinted with the permission of Sheed and Ward Limited.

Library of Congress Cataloging-in-Publication Data

Fox, Douglas A., 1927–
  Meditation & reality.

  Bibliography: p.
  Includes index.
  1. Meditation. I. Title. II. Title: Meditation
and reality.
BL627.F685 1986   291.4'3   85-45459
ISBN 0-8042-0662-7

© copyright John Knox Press 1986
10 9 8 7 6 5 4 3 2 1
Printed in the United States of America
John Knox Press
Atlanta, Georgia 30365

Preface

Methods of meditation, based usually but not always on oriental systems, have recently become a preoccupation of many Western people. The reasons for this interest are many, and the goals sought are not uniform. Much research and analysis of the practice and consequences of meditation has proceeded, and much more is needed, but the present seems to be a good time to draw together some of the tentative conclusions of the work performed so far, and to expose the entire subject to a fresh philosophical and even theological scrutiny.

First, however, it may be helpful to indicate the outline of this book and to give some idea of its scope. We shall be concerned with a fairly broad range of practices which may all be called "meditation" and with the values, positive and perhaps negative, which these may have for us. The significance of the frequently discussed "altered states of consciousness" which some meditation may certainly induce in us will also concern us. For convenience, this rather large subject will be divided into digestible sections, as follows.

Because oriental traditions of meditation loom large in the popular interest today, we shall begin there. India is our starting point, and, while trying to avoid obscurity or unnecessary complexity, we shall outline some of the most important meditation traditions of that land. While it would be a mistake to imagine that every Indian, or even a majority of them, has spent much time abandoning the daily demands for survival in solemn search for the soul, certain Indians have contributed a great deal to the theory and practice of our subject. We must begin with a man of the fourth century (or thereabouts) named Patanjali who wrote an enormously important work which systematized a form of yoga. From him we shall learn some of the classic terms of Indian yoga and an outline of the classical Indian practice.

Then, still in chapter 1, we will turn to some Buddhist ideas and discover a few more exotic but important words. Tantra comes next—a way of thinking and of practice which influenced later Hinduism and Buddhism but which probably had, at first, a life of its own. It will teach us a way of viewing both body and mind that some of our contemporaries find useful.

In chapter 2 we shall move on to examine more closely a few particular devices and procedures, many of which are used in several different schools of meditation and all of which are important enough to deserve our understanding. Thus we shall glance at the use of mandala, mantra, mudra, movement, action, intellection, "just sitting" (or, to give it the Japanese name, *shikan-taza*), "total awareness," and worship. Where necessary, these terms will be explained.

By the end of chapter 2 we should have a reasonable command of many distinctively Eastern patterns and elements in meditation, and in chapter 3 we shall briefly explore some Western sources. Meditation has flourished, at times and in places, as strongly in the West as in the East, in both Jewish and Christian settings. We shall now, therefore, selectively sample a little of this offering, mainly concentrating on two illustrious saints: Ignatius and Teresa. Although there are some different emphases here, there is also much that is similar to what we will have found in the East.

Methods and ideas of major meditative traditions will by now have been sufficiently uncovered for our purpose, and we shall turn to analysis. Before we can consider the meaning and value of claims that are made for meditation in any or all of its forms, it seems useful to inform ourselves of some of the most valuable research recently done on the effect of meditation on the human organism, its mind and body. Chapter 4, then, explores a variety of studies and will touch upon the opinions of Sigmund Freud and other analysts of similar traditions, as well as studies of biofeedback, "split brain" and bimodal consciousness theories, physiology, and psychotherapy. Although this section may demand slightly more careful reading for those unfamiliar with the material, we shall aim at clarity.

With chapter 5 we reach the heart of this book. Some remarkable claims are made for the value and meaning of certain "altered states" and we shall examine these, sympathetically yet critically. We shall, for example, look at the assertion that certain states of consciousness introduce us to a new grasp of the truth about reality itself, or that there is a condition in which we "realize" our own universality. Further, we will think about the alleged superiority of subjectivism ("turning inward") to objectivism ("turning outward to face the world") as a way of discovering the basic truth of life, the claim that intuition is a higher mode of knowledge than that available to reason, and other controversial but interesting topics. We shall consider the possible influence of some common modern problems such as "ontological anxiety" (the fear of not existing) and "identity conflict" (the struggle to know who and what we are) on at least some interpretations of meditative experience.

After a short chapter 6 in which we review our questions and begin a constructive response, we turn to Christian theology for insights about our subject, since it has coexisted with both Eastern and Western forms of meditation for centuries and may be expected to have learned something. A little Jewish thought (from Martin Buber) will also be found in chapter 7.

Chapter 8 will try to summarize some of the conclusions which we believe emerge from our study, trying to identify what may be constructive and healthy, and what may be dangerous in meditation.

Quite finally there will be, as an epilogue, a story: a fantasy that tries to make, in a different way, a few of the most important points that have surfaced by the end of the book.

Meditation—the focusing and inward-turning of awareness, the concentration of mental energies that produces striking modifications of consciousness—is our subject. We shall examine its dominant methods, East and West, its claims of value, and its potential for good or ill in our lives.

I should like to acknowledge my gratitude to my family and to friends who have been encouraging throughout this enterprise, especially my colleague Professor Joseph Pickle, without whose encouragement the manuscript, even when finished, would have lain dormant. I am grateful, too, to The Colorado College, its administration and faculty, for permitting the use of some research funds and much time in this business.

Douglas A. Fox
Colorado Springs

For Margaret

Contents

I

Meditation

The Aim of Meditation

Some meditators, it must be admitted, have no very clear idea of what they intend to achieve by their discipline. They meditate because it is a way of being "different" or in the hope that it will do some vague and unspecified good. Such lack of purpose, however, is not common. Most meditators have a fairly definite end in view: the attainment of tranquility, the acquisition of power, the quickening of the intellect, or perhaps the discovery of an important truth about themselves or about the universe. But in general it may be said that the goal of much, if not most, meditation can be expressed in a single word: *wholeness*.

Our time has been called the "age of anxiety," but in being anxious it can hardly claim originality. To study the artifacts of early civilizations is to wonder whether there was ever an age when humans (or at least some of them) were not perplexed and troubled about the meaning and value of life, concerned to meet its perils in a constructive way. Playwrights and novelists of the modern era have exposed repeatedly an evidently pervasive human wish to amount to something, to *mean* something, and to be part of a great and dignified enterprise. But the more we know about ourselves, the less confident many of us are.

Psychologists, biologists, paleontologists, and a host of others, observing that our performance can be studied in terms of cellular or chemical phenomena, are prone to judge that an end is no more than its means, a product no greater than its process, and thus they reduce us to ambulating laboratories. Further, since the publication of the first theory of our physical evolution from some "lower" species, many have become uneasy that, should any evolutionary theory be true, we may not be the the favored creatures of a God but merely the end products of a sequence of events that lacks rhyme or reason, ignoble in its beginning and its end. Kilgore Trout's *Venus on the Half-Shell* parodies this dismay by raising the vision of our life as having originated, bizarrely, in the ancient polluting of earth by visiting, intelligent cockroaches. These insects had come from another planet, one of many teams who had been sent out to take inventory of the universe. "They dumped their garbage and their excrement in the soupy primeval seas. . . . These contained microbes and viruses which flourished in the seas. . . . Life on these planets was an accident."[1] The hero of our story is badly shaken to discover that he is the end of a process that began so inauspiciously.[2]

Serious thought, of course, accounts for our beginnings differently, but not necessarily much more significantly, and many of us would like to find a truth about ourselves that rescues us from sheer meaninglessness. Among other philosophical and religious alternatives, meditation with its culmination in certain new kinds of consciousness sometimes presents itself as the way to such a truth. It promises further to offer us a way of living in the present without the haunting ghost of fear within us—a promise not to be despised in a time of such patent and enormous dangers as ours.

There is, moreover, an even more pervasive source of anxiety than those we have mentioned. We Westerners live in a rich and complex world. Inventiveness has multiplied gadgets to increase our comfort, entertain us, and maintain us in a steady state of desire. There are, in addition, a thousand competing claims every day to our attention and our loyalty, and we are stimulated by television, books, theater, education, rhetoric, and insurance salespersons until our minds are like trained seals, ready to jump through every hoop that presents itself. Indeed, we find ourselves worn ragged by our daily mental gymnastics, unable to focus for any length of time on any single idea. Our thoughts are like first graders on a playground, never still and hardly ever satisfactory.

The result of this mental diffusion is a more or less constant undertow of agitation, confusion, and fatigue. We become like a passenger on a small ship caught in a hurricane: all we really want is that the ship will hit some rock that will hold it still for a moment. Instead of the rich diversity of our culture bringing us happiness, we suffer as an overindulged child on Christmas morning—and, to make matters worse, like that same child we find usually that even our best toys grow stale after a few days, so that the energy spent in mastering them was largely wasted. Restlessly we seek more and more. We try to move faster and faster. Our grandparents spent the evenings slowly reading and chuckling over books, but we must learn to speed-read so that we can devour more and more books lest we die at last with one untasted. But the more we acquire and the faster we move, the more we fan the fires of our discontent.

Can we withdraw from this rat race? And in withdrawing, can we find some condition, some degree of poise in which a new and finer meaning can be discovered for our life, or in which the very concern for meaning is transcended?

Flight from confusion, from uncontrolled diversity, from panicky unfulfilledness: this, too, leads many to try meditation, for above all, meditation seems to promise peace. It offers a way of bringing our errant thoughts back to some gentle order, and it presents itself as a straight path to wholeness. We seek in it a truth—not so much a truth to know as a truth to *be*.

Because a fundamental source of our distraction and our frequent alarm lies in our experience of otherness, classic meditation authorities usually contend that our wholeness and peace entail the elimination of boundaries, the forgetting of distinctions. If one assumes that what causes distress must be, in some sense of the word, evil, and that evil must be less than truly real (since the real is good), it follows that the experience of unity within oneself which meditation may bring is the threshold of a unity that encloses the entire universe. Meditative experience, then, may become the experience of a boundless One in which there is neither clamor nor fear.

Some meditators, as we shall see, are theists: they believe that the final "Reality" which underlies all mere appearance is God, and that our peace and ultimate unity must therefore be in the experience of union with God. In meditation they seek the sense of being drawn into God, of dissolving the separation between God and themselves. Others, not being theists, seek not unity with a divine Person but simply a perfect stillness and a stopping of the frantic scurrying of one's own mind.

Some people find it comforting to know that meditation is not just another of the new and falsely lustrous gadgets of our time, but that good men and women have enjoyed it for millennia. It has the prestige of great age and great achievement to recommend it; only somewhat disturbing is our realization that it, too, presents us with diversity and a need for choice, since so many methods and philosophies of meditation have developed through the years. We would like to believe that this diversity is superficial, and that beneath it there may be a common core, a single body in a coat of many colors. To see if this is so, let us now briefly examine a few of those enduring hues.

Some Schools of Meditation

It is impossible to guess when people somewhere began to seek wholeness by methods we might today call "meditation" or when, by such methods, they enjoyed notably altered conditions of consciousness, but it is certain that one of the most influential eras in the development of this activity was around the fourth century A.D. It was then that someone known to us as Patanjali brilliantly drew together some earlier teaching and presented the world with the *Yoga Sūtra*, a more or less orderly body of instruction about the discipline and objectives of yoga. *Yoga* derives from the same root in the ancient Indo-European language system as the English term "yoke," and Patanjali's yoga may be thought of as a way of "yoking" the person who uses it to the final truth, bliss, and fulfillment of life.

The problem we face is that our mind is "unyoked." It is like an unruly ox that plunges about the field wildly and without restraint, serving no useful purpose and wearing itself out. As Patanjali might have put it, our mind or consciousness is undergoing modification all the time, never restfully savoring any one thing, never remaining still and firm, but passing through an endless parade of changes. We experience these modifications as dreams, hallucinations, memories, thoughts, perceptions, and misperceptions—in short, all our habitual mental activity, awake or asleep. The most unfortunate effect of this restlessness is that we become entrapped in our own thoughts, identifying ourselves with the images and assumptions of the mind and thinking ourselves to *be* the endless turbulence. In truth we are not like that at all. We are the deep ocean, not its surface waves. But we shall learn what we are and fully enter into our truth, becoming the perfect stillness of spirit itself (*ātman*) only when we learn to quieten the dancing mind, to restrain its modifications.

How, then, are we to find the peace we seek? The heart of Patanjali's method consists of learning to control awareness by fixing it firmly and unshiftingly on one thing, making it retain one modification rather than rushing from one to another. Concentration is the key to success in this enterprise, and the path to it has five stages.

We all find ourselves in stage one (*ksipta*, "the agitated") in which our thoughts fly from one object to another, and the retaining of just one idea or perception is quite beyond us. When we have worked hard at forcibly holding our awareness still, keeping a single thing in mind, we reach the second stage (*mūdha*, "the torpid") in which we become afflicted with a tendency to grow drowsy. There is some improvement by the third stage (*viksipta*, "the distracted") for here we have cultivated the power of concentration sufficiently to hold the mind briefly on one object. Even more progress has been made by the time we reach stage four (*ekāgra*, "the focused"), and now we can attend to a single object of thought for quite a long time; it is fair to say that we are now largely in control of our own mental processes. The climax of this entire effort is reached in stage five (*niruddha*, "the arrested"), when all movement of consciousness is suspended; without our becoming *un*conscious, nevertheless, we are perfectly still. Since most of the followers of Patanjali would hold that the truth about us and about all reality is that we are fundamentally a perfect calmness of undisturbed spirit, we are now ready for that "yoking" of ourselves to that truth. We are ready to *be* the unmoving, untroubled, eternally unruffled spirit that is quite beyond the possibility of danger or diminishment.

The final development—the attainment of a complete union or oneness with the pure, intrinsic spirit that is reality itself—comes only when we use our developed power of full concentration to focus upon the proper object, and this is no other than that spirit (*ātman*) itself.

Patanjali has offered us a method of progressively effective concentration of attention, and since he recognizes how far most of us stand from the attainment to which he points, he teaches also that there are some useful means which can help us to make progress. These are often called the "eight limbs" of yoga and they consist of teachings about the correct forms of behavior for one who would achieve deep meditation. Since these limbs are the bases on which many modern systems build their techniques, it will be worth our while to see just what they are like.

The "Eight Limbs" of Patanjali's Yoga

One must not think of the items that follow as progressive steps which must be perfected one at a time. All of them may be worked on simultaneously, although the beginner should certainly concentrate chiefly on the first few.

(1) *Yama*, or self-restraint. Here the seeker vows, and tries to achieve, certain kinds of restraint in his or her daily behavior. The particular virtues to be cultivated are (a) non-violence, (b) avoidance of lying, (c) avoidance of theft or misappropriation of anything, (d) restraint of the craving for sensual enjoyment, and (e) non-possessiveness. This last means that we must learn to live with simplicity and without the least luxury. A false yogin can be recognized by his enjoyment of unnecessary things and his acceptance of unnecessary gifts.

Yama does not aim at some mere moralism, but rather at helping us to loosen the ties that bind us to the world of fancies, unprofitable temptations, and illusions. The avoidance of misappropriation does not mean simply that we desist from stealing, as some commentaries seem to suggest, but that we withdraw ourselves from the daily temptation to take as our own all sorts of things that ought to be of no interest to us, such as honors and rewards which our community might wish to confer, or even the praise and adoration of our associates. In *yama* we are trying to get rid of all those behaviors which normally feed our ego.

(2) *Niyama*: rules of conduct. Where the items of *yama* were expressed negatively—as things to avoid—we have here some positive virtues that are to be cultivated. Again there are five: (a) Purity: this means keeping the body and mind clean of unwholesome tarnishings, and developing such traits as kindness, cheerfulness, and indifference to the faults of others. One should keep the body clean by bathing as often as is required, and one should be careful of diet, eating only foods that do not dull the mind. (b) Contentment under all circumstances. (c) Austerity: this entails some fasting and self-denial, and also a deliberate cultivation of contrition for any failures we may have allowed to occur in our progress toward the ideal. (d) Study of spiritually profitable books, and examinations of ourselves in the light of the knowledge gained from them. (e) Finally, thoughts of God and surrender to Divine will.

(3) *Āsanas*: the mastering of suitable bodily postures. Since the untutored body becomes uncomfortable if it is held in any position for too long, and since this discomfort dissolves our mental concentration, we must school the body to sit in some way that aids meditation. A number of acceptable *āsanas* are available, but all require practice and some are difficult at first to achieve. The real objective here is not to learn a tricky way of sitting, by means of which we may win the admiration of our less dexterous friends, but simply to learn to set our body in some way that will prevent the consciousness of our body and its demands from disturbing our concentration.

(4) *Prānayāma*: the control of breath. It is argued that as our breathing becomes properly measured and steady, so our minds tend to follow its example. As with posture, however, this "limb" needs the guidance of someone who is already a master.

(5) *Pratyāhāra*: the withdrawal of our senses from any objects. Here we learn *not* to pay attention to the sights, sounds, odors, feelings, and tastes which normally distract us and to focus all our attention inwardly.

(6) *Dhāranā*, or "retaining." This means keeping some object of attention before us without wavering and without allowing any second object to intrude and diffuse our focus. The mind is now set upon a single thing.

(7) *Dhyāna*: concentration. When our *dhāranā* skill is so per-

fected that we can hold the single object in attention without effort, we have attained *dhyāna*.

(8) *Samādhi*: perfect knowing. Even in the condition called *dhyāna* there is a measure of separation within our consciousness because the mind, in the act of knowing its object, also knows that it knows. In *samādhi* this separation has been overcome. The knower is not self-consciously knowing. Rather, the knower, the known, and the act of knowing are all one, and our mind is a stillness which becomes perfect.

Here is the essence of Patanjali's system. He gives us a goal and a method. The goal is a perfect unity of consciousness in which all disturbing distinctions such as self and other have been excluded, and the method is an arduous path of physical and mental discipline. But let us especially note that the center of all this is *concentration*—centering our awareness upon awareness itself progressively, until only pure consciousness remains. Those who attain this condition of mind will, of course, have to return to normal awareness in due course, but not without being refreshed and feeling that they have, for a moment, discovered their true being.

In Patanjali we find one of the really seminal teachers of meditation, one of the principal sources of the variety of practices called by that name today, but in addition to Patanjali's Indian *yoga* there are two other springs from which the waters of meditation have recently flowed. One of these is Buddhism, and the other is Tantra.

Buddhist Meditation

The Buddha, as a young man, became sensitive to what a modern existentialist might call the "absurdity" of our human experience. We suffer, grow old, and die. Nothing we achieve can survive forever. Nothing we cherish is imperishable. Indeed, as he saw the life of human beings to be largely an indefatigable quest for what can never be theirs—for permanence, security, and lasting happiness—he likened the world to a burning house and wondered how we could imagine ourselves content in it for even a moment.

Unlike some other Indian teachers, the Buddha did not believe that we could seek escape from our troubles in a God or in an immortal soul within us. These refuges were both unproven and unprovable and therefore illusory hopes. But peace *is* possible, he reasoned, for those of us who will combine the acceptance of a few fundamental truths with the practice of a distinctively Buddhist form of meditation. The truths are simply that existence cannot for long be enjoyed without suffering, that suffering arises because we ignorantly and foolishly allow ourselves to be filled with desire, that desire can be extinguished, and that the method for this overcoming of our otherwise insatiable longing is the Buddhist path of discipline.

Buddhism offers, from a point very early in its development, two main meditative procedures. Perhaps we should pause here to note that Buddhism is not a simple thing, but a very complex one, and we are not at this stage discussing such late and exotic forms of it as Zen and Tibetan religion. We may refer to these later, but for the present we shall confine ourselves to what would seem to be the older and more central teachings about meditation within Buddhism, and these concern themselves with two forms of meditation: absorptive or *jhāna*, and insightful or *vipassanā*.

Jhāna

Imagine yourself (if, indeed, this requires imagination) to be harried, harassed, and despairing. You feel that nothing in your life has ever gone quite as it should, nothing has ever really given all the satisfaction it promised, and your prospects for the future are painted in flat gray as far as the eye can see. You consult the Buddha. All you want is happiness—surely not too much to expect in a life you do not remember asking for.

The Buddha is kind (at least so long as you do not try to make him answer questions he has declined to discuss), and he tells you that your trouble is that you are a bundle of confused clingings—clinging to life, to hope in tangible attainments, to convictions about your immortality and worth, and so on. You must put such things out of your mind and learn to command your consciousness in a way that will bring it into the clear light of unconfused tranquility, desireless and illusionless. This sounds acceptable to you, so you ask how to proceed.

The objective in *jhāna* is to transform our consciousness, but we must begin where we are. We are incapable of concentrating for very long on anything, partly because our attention is constantly following our desires and rushing off on one mad errand after another. So we must learn to hold it still, and to enable us to do this we are given some object upon which to concentrate. This may be a blue circle or a candle flame or almost anything. If the Buddha feels that we need to be disenchanted with regard to the glory of a physical existence, he may even recommend that we spend a day in a cemetery, focusing our attention on a worm-eaten corpse. Generally, however, something like a blue circle will suffice.

Taking our blue circle with us, we retreat to some quiet spot, set the object before us, and begin to concentrate on it, trying not merely to maintain awareness of it, but at last to purge our mind of anything else so that our consciousness becomes nothing more than an awareness of the blue circle.

Through concentrating on our chosen object we shall, in time, learn to master the four degrees or stages of meditation that belong to what is called "the realm of form." That is, we begin by striving to exclude all but the blue circle from our attention, and we soon discover that the energy we must expend in this effort is enormous, so prone to wander is our mind. But at last we can focus our attention, although we are aware of the effort to do so. We can manage, finally, to close our eyes so that we no longer actually *see* our blue circle, but simply *think* it persistently. When we can do this we have mastered the first stage of our meditation.

The second degree of attainment comes when we can fill our mind with the meditation object and hold it steady there without conscious effort. This achievement, it is commonly reported, produces a sense of elation, of rapture and bliss. We are also aware of having a "collected" mind, and that is a very satisfying thing to have.

However, as we continue our concentrative discipline day after day, we finally dispel the rapture (stage three) and the bliss (stage four), since these were imperfections from the point of view of that unbreakable tranquility we seek.

When we reach the point of effortlessly holding a single object in mind without even the emotions that first accompanied this attainment, we are at the end of the four stages of meditation belonging to the "realm of form." That is, we have reached the point at which we will no longer need even the imagination of our blue circle, the "form" that helped us to concentrate our attention up to this time.

In stage five (the first of what are called the "formless" meditations), we try to imagine a limitless reality of nothing but empty space. What is other than ourselves, what is external to us, we think of no longer as a multiplicity of planets and stars, of trees and rivers, of promises and politicians, but simply as empty space.

When the empty space mind becomes easy for us, we move to stage six, in which we obliterate even that mental content and begin to become conscious of consciousness itself, and of that alone. This might seem to be as far as we can go in tranquilizing the mind, but it is not. In this state we are still divided. We are conscious *of* something (namely, consciousness itself), and that means that we are not yet so entirely unified that disturbance is impossible.

Thus we move to stage seven, when in place of a consciousness of consciousness we try to realize the idea that "there is nothing." This is a state of non-perception, a state in which we have passed beyond all ideas that arise from our sensory experience and the memory of it. But even this is not the end of our road, for there is stage eight: the condition which is called "neither-perception-nor-non-perception." Here we are alert but aware neither of any thing nor of any "nothing." We have a condition of simple awareness. We are awake, but the mind is unimaginably still.

It will readily be appreciated that the *jhāna* trail is a long and arduous one, and Buddhists have often conceded that it may take many lifetimes to perfect even one of the stages. In a system of thought that believes we can have as many lifetimes as we need, leisurely progress has not been a problem.

Today, however, many Buddhists feel the need to achieve their goal more quickly. There is some diminishing of confidence in the doctrine of rebirth and, in any case, the idea that our tranquility—the prelude, by the way, to the final deliverance from this mortal coil—is remote has led to the seeking of a shorter route. Fortunately, one is available in the *vipassanā* mode of meditation. This was traditionally thought of rather as a concomitant of the *jhāna* way, but since one can do it without any *jhānic* accomplishments there are some who turn directly to it as the speedy way to peace.

Vipassanā

Vipassanā meditation is intended to lead us beyond mere tranquility into the insight that life is exactly as the Buddha described it (filled with frustration and suffering, impermanent and soulless). Such an insight or intuition would itself herald our final liberation from illusion and desire, and therefore from the otherwise inevitable recurrence of despair.

The main tool of *vipassanā* is "right mindfulness," which has two ingredients: "bare attention" and "clear comprehension."

When, in our ordinary state of mind, we perceive things, we immediately respond to them with some value judgment. A flavor is delicious or unpleasant, a shape is aesthetically pleasing or ugly, and so on. Every time we respond like this we reinforce our prejudices and preferences, and strengthen our quite false sense of identification with them. We deceive ourselves through habit that we are particular and utterly unique persons because we embrace this set of judgments and tastes.

What we need to cultivate is the ability to perceive objects while remaining utterly without value judgments concerning them. That kind of perception is what the Buddhist means by "bare attention." It is attention unclothed in any of our prejudices. It is a purely receptive state of mind in which we simply accept our perceptions without registering any emotional response that favors or rejects them. A beautiful woman or a handsome man is seen simply as a fact, not an attractive fact. In this way we clean our mind of its assumptions and loosen the grip that our ego has on us.

Bare attention opens the way for "clear comprehension," a true understanding of the nature of all existence as so characterized by impermanence, so devoid of intrinsic value, that desire for it or for anything within it is naturally starved out of being.

A medical student of whom I heard during my college days had determined not to become entangled in marriage until he had completed his internship. He was no recluse, however, and every time he met a lovely woman he forced himself to see her as so many feet of intestine. He wanted to be able to associate with others without emotional entanglement. We may say that he was trying to practice a strangely modified form of bare attention, but I am not aware that it ever brought him clear comprehension.

To see every object without enchantment, without imposing a value upon it, is to relate to it with clarity and without either fear or hope. If we can do this, we weaken the hold on us of our usual set of emotions and shake ourselves free from the mistaken idea that each of us is a real, lasting, valuable "self" which can be recognized precisely because it always likes this and dislikes that, enjoys one thing and is afraid of another. What we usually mean by the pronoun "I" is not what we think it is at all. Our "I" is usually no more than a set of borrowed tastes, learned responses, acquired habits. So if we stop identifying with those tastes, responses, and habits, whatever we truly are will be set free to be itself.

Bare attention, the unclouded, unattached, pure observation of things, is the heart of *vipassanā* and the high road to a clear comprehension of things as they truly are. But such undistorted attention is not easy to achieve. Our assumptions can be very, very hidden indeed, and our likes or dislikes so subtle that we do not recognize their functioning to misshape our perceiving. *Vipassanā*, then, must offer us some objects on which to practice bare attending.

Since our most relentless valuing is usually of ourselves, *vipassanā* may often encourage us to use our own physical or mental functions as objects with which to strive for bare attention. If we can see that there is nothing either good or bad about each of these functions, and that none of them proves the existence of an immortal soul or self, our interest may become detached from the functions themselves and from the body that performs them.

Most commonly we may begin our *vipassanā* by attending to our own breathing. The technique is to sit quietly and observe one's respirations without trying to alter them in any way. One must try to become single-mindedly aware of the rising and falling of one's breast so that every breath is without any enduring significance but is fully known and attended to as *that respiration*. While it endures, it fills the awareness but evokes no emotion.

Eventually we should manage not to be aware of being aware of our breathing; we should, so to speak, have become nothing but the breathing. What we had at first objectified so that we could observe it has become finally, simply, one with our mind. We do not think about breathing, or critically analyze the way in which it is happening; each of us becomes a mere breathing itself.

By such means as this, we learn at last no longer seriously to think "I am breathing," but "there is breathing" or "breathing exists." If we are successful in this, the conviction of being a self slowly withers away. Then there is nothing for us to defend, nothing for us to fear, for there is no fragile self of which we are conscious and whose spurious needs we spend our time trying to supply. Consciousness itself, thought itself, becomes merely a fact unassociated with any sense of "my" or "mine."

This road, if followed faithfully, should lead us to a point beyond the causes of "our" suffering, not merely to peace but to that which is quite beyond anything we could imagine the word "peace" to mean. It will bring us to *nirvāna*, the "extinguishing" of all that is awry, all that is disjointed and vulnerable in existence.

Nirvāna, the "blowing out" of the fires of desire and involvement, is usually thought of as the end of Buddhist meditation. Sometimes, however, a further stage is mentioned about which very little can clearly be said. It is called *nirodh* (comparable to the *niruddha* of Patanjali), and the Buddhist describes it as the total cessation of awareness in any form.

In the condition of *nirodh* even the meditator's physical functions seem to be suspended, and one might easily be mistaken for a corpse except that one's body does not decay. This state might last, apparently, for quite a long time. It is reasonable to surmise that physical functions such as breathing and heartbeat are not actually suspended, but operate at such a minimal level that only sophisticated instruments can easily detect them.

The third great wing of Indian meditation lies in the tradition known as Tantra, which plays a part in some of the meditative techniques offered today.

Tantra

The approach to life and illumination known as Tantra is a very rich thing. It has evoked vitriolic denunciation and fanatical defense, and it has been largely misunderstood—not only in the West, but among very many Easterners as well. If we were bent upon a responsible, scholarly study of Tantra for its own sake, we would have to begin by disentangling the Buddhist from the Hindu elements in the tradition, and then proceed to a close analysis of methods, metaphysics, and localized manifestations. Happily, none of this need detain us, for it is only the kind of central conviction that Tantra offers meditators today that concerns us, and this we may deal with quite shortly.

Tantrists, like other meditators, are concerned to achieve wholeness and to find the best method for unifying the many polarities of our experience. They are often disenchanted with rival types of discipline, because these seem to be based on an incomplete view of what we are. Many meditation systems, from the viewpoint of Tantrists, force the body into a state of mere quiescence because the great interest is in the manipulation of mental activity. But we *are* a body, and if wholeness is to be achieved it must come by means of the body, not in spite of it. The general Tantric tendency, then, is to use the body as a means to our fulfillment.

When we speak of Tantra and the use of the body, many people begin to smirk salaciously, remembering vague stories about the orgiastic use of sex. Sexuality is, indeed, a reality that Tantra uses, but there have been gross misunderstandings of the role played by sexual contact in this system. In fact, sexual ritual is not the aspect of Tantra that is seriously influencing many Westerners at present, so we could safely ignore it, but it may be worthwhile to get a truer perspective.

The fact is that true and responsible Tantrists have never been libertines. On the contrary, they have tended to conduct themselves with a restraint that would have done credit to a Puritan. Sexual practices enter their repertoire only after a very high degree of self-control has been achieved, and then only in the case of a select few adepts. Of course, there have been Tantric sects considerably less responsible than the best (evidently the Kaula sect is an example), but even here the reputation for sexual indulgence is almost certainly exaggerated.

Sexual encounter is, in any event, only one way in which a duality may be overcome and a union experienced. As a matter of fact, unless we are already deeply advanced in the attainment of wholeness, our sexual adventures tend not to be unifying at all, but to express our selfishness and our personal imbalance. They may lead to a moment of pleasure and the release of tension, but this moment is a very brief one and essentially unsatisfying because it has nourished our egoism, not our love. It has been merely an instance of our exploitation of someone else (who was doubtless exploiting us as shamelessly at the same time). So Tantra is not interested in sexuality for its own sake, and can make use of it effectively only after other methods for unification of our personality and the transcending of tensions and polarities have had considerable success. It is among these other methods that we must look for the contribution Tantra may make to Western meditation today.

Tantric psychology regards the human body as a model, in miniature, of the universe—a microcosm. Thus, as our earth receives light and energy from the sun and moon, so our bodies are thought to be influenced by currents of force that complement each other and are called "solar" (*sūrya-svarūpa*) and "lunar" (*candra-svarūpa*). The solar energies of the body vivify our intellectual activities, our powers of discrimination, and our tendency to set things in their place, to classify and analyze, and to perceive ourselves as different from all other things. In other words, the solar energies within us are centrifugal— they tend to diffuse us. Our consciousness becomes a consciousness of many objects, and we know ourselves as one more object among the rest. Our lunar forces, on the other hand, empower certain unconscious processes whose tendency is centripetal—drawing us in and unifying our consciousness. Love is a product of these energies, and so is everything that causes us to put together again what the intellect has set apart.

Obviously, we shall remain in tension so long as the forces within us are working against each other rather than in harmony. Further, we are tense because we experience our own individuality, our personal selfhood, as in conflict with a vaguely longed-for cosmic unity. There is, thus, a duality of personal spirit and divine Spirit which, like all dualities, discomforts us. How are we to create unity within ourselves?

Indian and Tibetan (Buddhist) Tantra both make use of a set of images that aid in achieving the unifying of the mind and body, the particular spirit and the cosmic, and all the other pairs of opposites of which our reality seems to consist. Indian systems (represented most popularly by Kundalini Yoga) often seem to treat these images as if they were literally accurate, while Tibetans seem, on the whole, not to care so much whether we are describing actual things or merely convenient fictions. The procedures of both, however, are significantly similar.

Imagine that there is a hollow channel running through your spine, passing through a series of sensitive "centers" (*cakras*), the lowest of which is near the base of your spine and the highest of which is at the top of your head. The number of these *cakras* differs in the Buddhist and the Hindu systems.

Coiled in sleep at the base of this channel is a great creative force (something like Freud's *libido*), which we may think of as a serpent. It is called Kundalini and, in addition to everything else, it represents the female aspect of the cosmos, the consort of the cosmic deity. Somehow we must awaken the Kundalini, causing it to uncoil and move itself up the spine's channel (the *susummā*) until, having passed through each of the *cakras* in turn, it finally reaches the apex of the body and there unites with the male deity, flooding us with illumination and bliss in a moment of total and dynamic unification.

Each of the *cakras* through which the Kundalini is thought to pass on its upward journey is representative of an experience of relative illumination which the meditator or yogin will enjoy as he or she learns to move the formerly dormant power within.

If it can be assumed that what is achieved in the microcosm is simultaneously perfected in the macrocosm—that the subjective unification we experience within us is matched by our unification with all reality—it is hard to think of a more rewarding goal. Chintaharan Chakravarti writes that

> a careful and sympathetic study of the literature will . . . go to show that the ideal of the Tantras is the realisation of the identity of the Individual Soul with the Supreme Soul. And the various rites in tantric worship will be found on a close study to be so conceived as to help this realisation in a graduated scale.[3]

Here, then, is a vision of wholeness indeed! There are various

methods that accompany these images, and about some of them little is
known because they are felt to be safe only in the hands of a thoroughly
experienced master. Representative of Tantric procedures is a respira-
tory technique described by Lama Anagarika Govinda.[4]

We are asked to imagine two channels, or *nādīs*, one of which
begins with our left nostril and the other with our right. They coil
around our spine until they make contact with the *susummā*, or
Kundalini's channel, at the base of the spine.

With this image in mind, envision yourself feeding certain syllables associated with the vowels of the Sanskrit alphabet into the left of
these *nādīs*, and others associated with the consonants into the right.
Since these syllables represent all that exists in the universe, we are in
effect consciously driving reality itself through our bodies in two
streams which, upon reaching the point at the base of our spine where
Kundalini lies, awaken this latent power and induce it to rise, as it
were, almost as if it were borne upward by them as they fuse at the
point of meeting and thrust it before them.

One Tantric method, then, consists of a concentration of mind
and will upon a process associated with our breathing; it is pictured as
the slow drawing upwards through our body of a power which fulfills us
as it reaches its climax in the perfect infiltration and unifying of our
whole being.

We have by no means exhausted the kinds of meditation that
India has produced, nor have we discussed all that are appearing on the
Western scene today. Tibetan religion is replete with additional ideas
and methods, some of which will certainly seem to the uncommitted
more fanciful than inspired; methods based on Chinese, Japanese, or
other traditions (particularly Zen) have their own coloration.

Conclusion

Among the systems of meditation offering themselves to us today, some representative Indian ones aim at a sense of wholeness
within ourselves and, sometimes at least, a sense of having achieved a
sort of unity with all reality. They do this most conspicuously by disciplines that achieve a concentration of the attention, a focusing of
awareness, whether by using some device such as an image or an idea,

or by directing attention to a process which is thought to be going on inside us.

Our consciousness and our entire personality is ordinarily like a kindergarten class that has scattered itself over a hillside in pursuit of a hundred butterflies. The wise teacher does not try to capture each single child by main force and drag it back to wherever it should be (although a little of that may be necessary, too). Rather, the teacher finds something engrossing, places it where he or she would like the children to gather, and merely finds a way to draw attention to its presence. The children will finally gather of their own accord.

Meditators, therefore, do not usually try to belabor every wandering thought and impulse. Rather, they raise for their own attention something upon which to focus, something capable of engaging the entire mind. They allow their attention to gather itself around this target, and thus in time they learn to be relatively collected. The precise nature of the target—a blue circle, breathing, emotional processes, Kundalini, or whatever it may be—may not be a matter of first importance after all. A sense of wholeness comes when we are absorbed and concentrated; it is perfected when the absorption is complete so that the very process of being aware of what absorbs us is ended.

But the "drawing in" of our attention requires much practice, and over the centuries various meditational schools have developed additional devices and methods to help us.

2

Some Elements of Method

We have seen that concentrating or focusing attention is one of the most characteristic features of meditation. The goal of this effort is a special kind of awareness which is free from the distraction and diffusion of our customary mental life. We seek to be "centered" or to be "collected" and to find a stillness in which we may discover a new understanding of ourselves and our place in the universe. Most of the time our thoughts are like the surface of a very choppy sea, and in meditation we want to sink down into the depths.

Because our mind runs panting after every sensory impression it receives, one of the things meditators must learn to do is to shut off the ceaseless flow of these. The skill required to achieve this is, however, acquired only with practice, and in the meantime our senses may be used in various ways which will help to gather the splaying fringes of our attention and focus them.

The use of virtually every sort of sensory experience to help concentrate attention has led to the development of some methods and devices that are worth our brief notice, since some of them are the most commonly familiar elements of popular meditational systems. Regarding mantras, mandalas, mudras, and other devices, however, a word of warning may be useful. Certainly, these are all useful tools of concentration. Such is the human penchant for imposing superstition on the mundanely psychological and for substituting the titillation of the exotic for the stimulus of authentic mystery, however, that many of these tools have been invested by some tradition with the aura of some extraordinary and intrinsic power. Particular mandalas and mantras, for example, are thought by some to contain or express a distinctive force that makes them either especially efficacious or, for the unworthy, dangerous to use. This is a belief that need not command our unqualified respect.

Mandala

The first instrument of meditation which we should recognize is the mandala. The use of this instrument has had wide acceptance, especially in the Far East, and some Jewish and Christian symbols have, at times and for some people, had a mandala-like function.

The word *mandala* is a Sanskrit term meaning "circle," and, strictly speaking, it means a circular pattern intended to summarize and express symbolically the character of the cosmos and human wholeness. Hinduism and Buddhism have made extensive use of mandalas as objects upon which to fix the gaze and concentrate the thought.

It would take an entire book to do justice to the arrangements of deities, Buddhas, and other figures that are to be found in various mandalas and to explore the often subtle significance of the designs, but it is enough for us to recognize the *function* of these pictures. No doubt their seed lies in much simpler objects used for focusing attention—such as the blue circle alluded to in our last chapter—but their value lies partly in the fact that they are not only capable of becoming the single object that fills and stills the mind, but they are also symbols of a particular metaphysics. They can represent a view of the universe and of life which, as it is progressively understood by the earnest meditator, can shape attitudes and responses. Any striking change in the state of the meditator's psyche, since it takes place in connection with the mandala and its meaning, will be felt as an "awakening" to the truth of that meaning, and even as a confirmation of it.

Mandalas are very potent tools for transforming our reactions to all the circumstances of life. They not only help us to quieten the mind and calm the spirit as we control our mental life by fixing our attention, but they help (through their esoteric meaning) to build up in us a mind-set that interprets our experience.

In short, a mandala is a meaningful design that may be used both to assist us in concentrating our attention and in shaping the underlying values and concepts of our life.

Mantra

If we had only one sense, vision, we might need nothing more than mandalas to aid our meditation. In fact, however, our hearing also feeds distraction to our mind, and it is therefore inevitable that sound should provide another kind of instrument for concentration.

A mantra is a sound that is used to facilitate the narrowing of our attention. The word itself seems to be derived from a root, *man*, which refers to thinking, and another, *tra*, which is usually an element in words alluding to an instrument. A mantra, then, is an instrument of thinking, and in some extremely idealistic systems of thought in which the entire world is considered to be only a sort of "idea" (either God's or ours), a mantra is a word that may be considered capable of bringing things into existence.

More commonly, however, the mantra is a syllable, a word, or a phrase whose repetition focuses our thought and helps to bring about some desired state of mind. Thus, the Krishna Consciousness cultist rhythmically chants "Hare Krishna, Hare Krishna, Krishna, Krishna, Hare, Hare, Hare Rama, Hare Rama, Rama, Rama," and hopes thereby to attain a condition of ecstatic union with Krishna, the Lord. If the cultist is successful, he or she feels wonderfully liberated from all the troubles of this world, even from the body itself. Or the devotee of the Soka Gakkai movement chants *Nam myoho renge kyo* (which may roughly be translated "Praise to the Lotus Sutra") and feels that this phrase carries with it the very rhythm of the universe, so that by properly chanting it one not only achieves a concentration otherwise impossible, but puts oneself in tune with all reality.

In more sophisticated systems than these, the meaning of the mantra is unimportant. It may even be valuable not to know what the word or sound means, because if we do we may be led astray into thinking about that meaning instead of letting all discursive thought cease as our mind becomes absorbed by the sound itself. In Indian traditions the greatest mantra is the syllable *Om*, and its value lies partly in the fact that its meaning is so universal and all-inclusive that it eludes formulation. Nothing is excluded from *Om*, so there is no point in assigning a particular meaning to it or letting the mind idly speculate about it. It serves as the ideal link between the meditating individual and the absolute reality with which that person seeks to be identified in his or her own experience. To be totally absorbed in *Om* is to be lost to all sense of individuality, to be liberated from the limits of selfhood.

Some traditions place great emphasis on pronouncing the mantra properly. Others, however, laugh at such finicky precision and point out that mantras "work" however they are pronounced, provided the spirit of the recitation is correct. Lama Anagarika Govinda, a German expatriate and a notable member of a Tibetan religious order, has some luminous remarks on this subject. He points out that if the exact pronunciation of mantras were important, then all those borrowed by Tibet from India would be useless, because the Tibetan has never pronounced them as an Indian would.[1] Making the same point is a charming story recounted by John Blofeld. A monk in Yunnan told about an ignorant man who had been given a mantra to recite. In English the mantra would have meant roughly "O, the Jewel in the Lotus," and referred to the Buddha. However, the semi-literate chanter misread one of the Chinese characters in which this formula had been written for him and spent months saying "O, the Jewel in the Lotus Ox." This, of course, is a rather silly phrase, but it gave our hero great satisfaction and he felt that his character was definitely being spiritualized by his chanting. When he met again the monk who had prescribed the mantra, our rough enthusiast recited it to show how well he had practiced. The monk, predictably, laughed aloud, then, kindly, corrected his student's pronunciation. For some time the good fellow recited the formula correctly, but to his disgust he found that it did not now achieve for his consciousness the same marvelous results that he had enjoyed with his Lotus Ox, and in despair he betook himself to the master for consultation. The monk listened to the complaint, thought a moment, and then said, "All right. You had better repeat it in the old way. It is not the words which count but the mental attitude."[2]

Mudra

In addition to sights and sounds, physical postures and gestures may be helpful foci of attention. This brings us to the device known as mudra or "sign." Essentially a mudra is a symbolic gesture, thoroughly stylized and usually performed with the hands or fingers. Indian dances make great use of such gestures that convey a meaning to the educated audience, and meditation also resorts to mudras as a means of fixing the mind.

There is a considerable repertoire of hand positions in Hinduism and Buddhism, any of which may be adopted to facilitate our narrowing of attention as well as our expressing some conviction that will support our meditation. Up to the present time, mudras seem to have won less favor among Western meditators than have either mantras or mandalas.

Movement

Many people who long for the sense of being "centered" and poised, who regret the wild profusion of their interests and thoughts, the chaos of their lives, nevertheless reject any kind of meditation that requires them to sit still. We are, after all, not merely processes of thought. We are a psychosomatic unity, a togetherness of physical and mental life, the mental dependent on the physical for its very existence. Moreover, we are not blocks and stones that happen to have started rolling when they ought to be sedately gathering moss; we are muscles, nerves, an intricate and wonderful machine designed for movement. Does this not mean that to be *un*moving in body or thought is in some way to be untrue to ourselves? At least it is clear that pure stillness of body and mind is not the only way to be unified and at peace. To realize our truest and inmost reality may require, for some of us at least, not the suppression of motion, but a particular way of disciplining ourselves in and by motion.

Dance and other forms of deliberate movement become, for many persons, means toward the goal of centered wholeness. The myths of India give to dance an origin among the gods themselves, and since dance, as much as yoga, may induce ecstasy, trance, and the feeling of absolute unity within oneself and within the cosmos, it has become an important ingredient in Indian religion.

It is China, however, that seems to be providing Westerners with the most popular form of disciplined yet liberating movement available today, and an impressive number of instructors in *T'ai-chi Ch'uan* may be found in the yellow pages of major telephone books. *T'ai-chi*, as it is often called for short, has its most obvious roots in Taoism, a luxurious mixture of religion, metaphysics, and magic with a long history of fluctuating fortune in China. To the uninformed, *T'ai-chi* may look like a cross between slow-motion boxing and ballet and, indeed, it has something of each in it. It provides part of the basis for some oriental martial arts, but it may be as pacific as Parsifal.

A typical exercise in *T'ai-chi* is sometimes called the Willow Tree. Here one learns to move one's body in gentle and flowing circular movements in imitation of a willow which is swayed by the wind. The movement itself is useful as a means of focusing attention, but the ultimate achievement in *T'ai-chi* would come when a person had become such a unity of consciousness, movement, and identification with the tree as to have lost all preoccupation with the self and was instead experiencing himself or herself at one with nature. What is produced here, then, is at once a flow of graceful and unimpeded motion and a profound stillness of emotion in the absence of mental unrest.

Perhaps the most important contribution of the technique we are now discussing is the recognition that peace, fullness, and wholeness may not be identified too rigidly with pure and total stillness. There is a considerable philosophical issue at stake here that has been debated by thinkers of both West and East: is reality at its best at rest or in motion? If it is at rest, we have a problem to account for the experience of motion; if that which is most real is fundamentally movement or process, however, what is rest and why does it refresh us? Like Process Philosophy in the West, Taoism chooses to see reality as both being and becoming (or, in a sense, neither simply being nor becoming), as a flow as well as an "uncarved block;" it offers us the joy of movement as a pathway to our ultimate wholeness.

Let us make no mistake, however: movement of the kind we have described can serve the ends of meditation only so long as it ceases to be the expression of a self-consciousness, only as it becomes something in which we may lose ourselves, becoming unified and concentrated so that we are, as it were, simply the motion itself and not reflection about the motion. As much as with mantra or mandala, the meditative function of movement is a focusing, a centering of the whole self and an end of objective, discursive thought.

Action

Yet another possible tool of meditative absorption is action—virtually any kind of action, including our daily work, our acts of charity or domestic obligation, and even our play. If some may lose themselves and find peace through dance, others may do so through everyday activities. The trick is so to act that we become wholly contained in the acting itself, totally but unreflectingly involved in what we are doing so that the doing and the doer are one.

This means that we must not value the act in terms of its possible consequences. It must not matter to us whether what we are doing produces a successful result, or whether it ends in failure. It is the action itself that must engage us, and we must not think about "good" or "bad" outcomes; we must not prize some consequences more than others. To place a value on the result is to involve ourselves in a subtle form of self-esteem, because whenever we regard a consequence as "good" we mean "good for us" or "good by our standards." Let the results simply be what they will, and let us become wholly absorbed in the act itself. This is the way of *Karma-Yoga*, as Indian traditions name it, and it is one of the most readily available of all paths to selflessness and peace. It is, however, not yet one of the more popular techniques of contemporary Western meditators.

Intellection

Most of those who seek through meditation some profound illumination reject the idea that ordinary rationality can take us very far toward the truth they seek. Such a truth must usually be "seen" intuitively; it cannot be learned. It "comes" to us all at once when the proper degree of mental discipline, of concentrated awareness, has been achieved. This means that the machinery of conventional reasoning must somehow be slipped out of gear, and what is usually meant by the word "thought" must come to a temporary stop. Yet, paradoxically, reason itself may help to bring us to this happy pass, and conscious mental effort may be a tool for suspending mental effort.

It should be noted that not all meditators seek the sort of absolute stillness of reason that we have described above. Some aim at a condition in which the flow of thought goes on as before, but is "contained" in a larger sort of awareness, a kind of unmoving, perfectly comprehensive "knowing" that feels as if it were a vast Cosmic Mind being quite still and at rest yet also being aware of the movement of a molecule of reason within it. This is a condition in which one experiences both the process of thinking and a fancied (or actual) transcendence of thinking. It is a condition somewhat like our common capacity to observe ourselves thinking (I notice that I am thinking about this), except that the observing side of us has achieved a sort of distance from the side of us it is observing, and senses its own limitlessness.

Whichever of these conditions we may be seeking to enjoy, intellection can become a tool of our psychic self-manipulation. An example of the procedure we are trying to describe is the Rinzai Zen use of the device known as *koan*. A *koan* is a riddle whose solution lies outside the range of logic. No doubt the most famous of koans is the question, "What is the sound of one hand clapping?"

Pilgrims whose promised land is Zen *satori* (or awakening) may spend many hours puzzling about a *koan*. They may find many "answers" that seem to be satisfactory, but they will discover that the meditation master will reject them all—perhaps rather rudely. At last, if all goes well, the resources of reason will be utterly exhausted and the mind will throw up its hands in resignation. Reasoning comes to an end—for the moment. The content of the mind, the accumulated values, assumptions, chains of logic, and other things that culture and experience have used to encrust the pristine clarity of pure being within us fall away, and without learning anything new we simply and immediately see. The "Truth" is *there*, not to be grasped but simply to be known. And in knowing it we are at once the knower and the knowing and the known, for all differences, all distance, all distinctions have disappeared.

What, then, is the significance of the *koan*? It is essentially a sort of mantra: it is something that gathers our wandering attention, focuses it, narrows it until it is engaged unwaveringly with one question, and thus brings it to a still point where the movement of thinking is suspended. As we shall see later, it is the achievement of that unmoving and intense concentration that brings about, quite naturally, the "leap" beyond reason into what is accepted as a new and utterly different sort of consciousness.

In short, the *koans* of Zen, like the mantras of Transcendental Meditation or the mandalas of Shingon Buddhism, are essentially devices for concentrating the mind until a sort of "blink" occurs in which we seem to stand in a new relation to whatever exists. In this relation we no longer merely apprehend what we know but feel that in a wordless sense we *com*prehend it—gather it wholly within us so that there is no remaining separation between things, between subjects and objects, and so on. Concentration is the objective of this device, as it was of most others, and once again a tranquil wholeness is the goal ultimately sought.

Shikan-taza

Zen Buddhism has contributed another method to the armory of meditation, and it is one that is well worth our examining because it goes directly to the heart of things. It is called *shikan-taza* or, as this is often loosely translated into English, "just sitting."

If you believe that the anxieties and the hopes, the images of yourself and the values you treasure are all mere flotsam floating on the surface of your mind, and that beneath all these, bearing them up, the true *you* is a vast, deep ocean inseparable from all reality, you will want to experience that ocean and escape from the domination of the surface rubbish. All the methods we have discussed are designed to achieve this, but *shikan-taza* is perhaps the most direct, even if in some ways the most difficult, of all.

To do *shikan-taza* is to sit with extreme alertness and concentration of mind but *without ideas*. It is to be so extremely awake that any intrusive noise or other sensation is sharply recorded, yet to be quite without a flow of thought. It is a condition of alert non-thinking.

Obviously, this is much easier to prescribe than to perform, and a great deal of practice is required to master the art of *shikan-taza*. At first one is easily distracted by noise coming from the world around; but one must learn not to resist the noise and grow resentful of it. Rather, one tries to identify with the noise, to *become* the noise, so that the hearing subject loses itself in the heard object—then the opposition, the tension between subject and object, hearer and noise, disappears. Years ago I learned a little poem by the great Zen master Dogen, and although long since I have lost the source of it, I remember the poem:

> Hearing the raindrops on the roof,
> Here I sit, empty [of thought] with no mind.
> The raindrops splash—
> That is, the raindrops hear themselves.

In this somewhat cumbrous translation it is, I hope, clear that Dogen is describing a state of *shikan-taza*. He has been sitting without thought, without self-conscious perception of what was going on around him, while rain fell and dripped from the eaves of his hut. So successfully did he "become the sound" that it was as true to say that the raindrops heard themselves as to say that he heard them, for there was no Dogen in his consciousness, no separate identifiable self at all: there was only the one event, Sound-Hearing, not two events or two beings.

An analogy may help us to see what *shikan-taza* is like. If you think of our ordinary consciousness as a kind of mirror, reflecting all the things that appear before it, all the sense impressions and images, *shikan-taza* is the condition in which one has removed all the objects so that the mirror exists brightly, but without a single thing reflected on its surface. Others have said that the mind, in *shikan-taza*, becomes like a sheet of clean, white paper. The point is that all mental activities have been suspended, and one is simply *there*, intensely awake, but without the passage of any reflection or idea.

What is achieved by this state? Essentially the same thing that all successful meditation achieves: we are rescued from our frenzy, our dispersal over the whole landscape of our anxieties. We are made still, collected, with a sense of wholeness.

Why is there a sense of wholeness in this? The answer is simple. In our ordinary moments we are thinking about what we must do, planning our responses, working out advantageous behavior—there is nothing spontaneous in what we do at all, and this means that we are concealed behind a facade of ideas and fears and hopes and learned responses. To be simply oneself is to be spontaneous, but to be spontaneous is to be unreflective, to act immediately and out of what we are, not out of what we think will best serve some interest.

There are many stories of Zen masters suddenly striking a disciple or reaching out to twist an unsuspecting nose. Why did they do this? Because when we are injured we do not carefully reflect "I am in pain; I have been hurt; I will cry out!" We simply cry out. In forcing such a moment of immediacy and spontaneity upon their disciples, the masters often awakened them to the difference between just *being*, and hiding their true self behind a wall of ideas.

So in *shikan-taza* one simply sits, without mental operations, innocent of all scheming, all imagining, all hoping. One simply *is*.

This, too, is a kind of concentration, but we are not now using some object to help us focus, and that is why *shikan-taza* is one of the most difficult of all methods of meditation. We are concentrating our mental energies . . . on nothing! When this procedure is successful, it, like all the other methods we have discussed, will bring to us a sense of release from troubled diffusion of interest and of selfhood; it will give us inner stillness, calmness, and peace. And, too, it will bring us to the "blink" in which we are quite suddenly aware of having stepped back from our old self-image, the encrustation of old acquired manners, and into a feeling of freedom simply to be whatever we really are.

But let us beware of one mistake: *shikan-taza* may be said to be a "mindless" sitting. If this means that it is without the distraction of active reflection, that is an accurate description. But it is not mindless in the sense of dull, stupid, or sleepy. I have often observed my students assume what is evidently a mindless condition during some flood of my eloquence, but it was by no means *shikan-taza* that occupied them.

Total Awareness

In one way or another the meditation methods we have considered so far have aimed at a narrowing of attention in order to achieve focus and concentration. Sometimes, however, a meditative system may make use of an almost completely opposite technique: the striving for a kind of total awareness of the immediate environment.

Ordinarily our "seeing" is remarkably exclusive; we see only a fragment of the scene that really lies in front of us. Stage magicians rely heavily on this fact and know that if they can oblige us to attend to one thing that is happening, we can safely be trusted to ignore something else. We edit our sensory experience in accordance with wishes, fears, self-understandings, and a hundred other predispositions.

One way to break out of the prison of our limited self-consciousness, then, is not to select from the vast range of stimuli around us some *one* thing to occupy our attention exclusively, but to throw the mind open to the world in its fullness—or at least to that part of it which is within our perceptual range. Let us be fully and wholly engaged with what is before us.

To do this we must suspend our judgments of good and bad, acceptable and otherwise, and simply let each entity come to us. We must let ourselves be wholly "present" to each item that confronts us, and we must let each item be entirely itself for us, without the imposition of our values upon it. In short, instead of thinking about the world, we will *receive* the world, and our subjectivity will become calm in that unresisting and inclusive openness.

This sounds easy to do, but it is not. The habit of evaluating ("I love that sound," "That's my favorite color," "I can't stand the smell of raw sewage!") is so strong in us that we can hardly prevent our reception of the world from stimulating and becoming confused in feelings of attraction or repulsion. But it is essential that we put aside all our prejudices (however well-founded we think them to be) and simply accept with all our attention. *With all our attention*: that is the critical phrase. We must be wholly aware of each stimulus as it comes to us, not greeting it with a fragment of a scattering attention, but accepting it with our fullest gaze, and then letting that gaze encompass and gather in other things, resisting nothing, but giving itself totally to each object in turn and finally to all together. It is the totality of the attention given that is critical, for it is in this unedited, unrushed awareness that we are personally concentrated and are given the impression of our own wholeness.

Here, then, is a method which seems expansive rather than concentrative. Because it aims at the gathering of our forces of consciousness, even though it allows these to engage many objects, it is not really so different from other methods we have considered; and it appears to lead, at last, to the same subjective results.

Worship

Finally, worship may be an element of meditative method. By this I do not mean the sort of thing that usually happens in a typical suburban church on Sunday morning. Whatever *that* is, it often has little to do with any recognizable meaning of the term "worship." Rather, I mean a sensitive and whole-minded appreciation of the presence of the embracing Mystery in which, as the Bible puts it, "we live and move and have our being" (Acts 17:28).

Adoration of God is the heart of true worship, and this means the self going out of itself in complete openness to Another. It is the response to the command, "Be still, and know that I am God" (Ps. 46:10). In brief, worship is the absorption of our entire attention in an awareness of That-who-is-to-be-adored. It is the finite person lost but not obliterated in love for the Infinite Person. Such a movement of our consciousness gathers us together, focuses our attention, concentrates our mind, and brings us to a sense of transcendent understanding and a profound peace. It, too, can produce the "blink" in which we slip out from beneath the weight of our former self-image (with its burden of guilt, insufficiency, and triviality) and acquire a new kind of identity and sense of wholeness.

Conclusion

What is the element common to all the methods we have indicated in this chapter? Is it not that all of them are concerned with the effort to concentrate psychic energy and firmly fix attention on that through which the discovery of our deepest self may come? Do they not all lead to the cessation of our usual aimless diffusion of attention? Clearly they are designed to still the restless mind and emotions, to attain a unified awareness; they may even bring to us the condition that is often described as "neither consciousness nor unconsciousness"—an alert tranquility without a radical sense of alienation between self and object. Even the theistic worshiper, focused adoringly upon his or her God, may so completely lose self-awareness in the overwhelming sense of the divine Presence as to be finally aware only of God and not of his or her own awareness of God.

All this means that the devices and techniques we have mentioned may well lead to a state of mind in which we have abandoned our former more or less constant, if subterranean, concern with ourselves as a vulnerable set of values and opinions. We may no longer even think in terms of "I" and "mine"—or, if we do, we may at least take ourselves a little less seriously as the centers of all value in the world—and this means that we may reach the place that most meditators, I believe, prize above all others: the state of freedom from fear and anxiety. After all, what is there to fear when there is no great concern in us for a limited and fragile "I"? How can we be anxious when we not only have everything we really need, but know ourselves actually to *be* everything that really is, or to be *at one* with God who is the single encompassing Reality?

Tantric Postscript

There is one meditative tradition that is inclined to be scornful of all others and, although it may use methods we have outlined, to do whatever it does with an attitude it thinks to be distinctive. This tradition is Tantra, of which we said a little in the last chapter. We should not end this chapter without a Tantric reservation or two about the use of *any* meditational method that is not supported by an adequate view of reality.

Much of the basic Tantric philosophy is curiously familiar to those who really understand the traditional philosophies of Judaism or Christianity, for there are some striking parallels, the most profound of which is the rejection of any simple, uncritical Monism—that is, any view that the world may usefully be regarded as a distinctionless One with no complexities at all.

Tantra, like a number of Western systems of thought, tends to discuss reality as composed, in some sense, of a set of dualities. Our personal sense of instability and our societal disorders are the results of the falling into disarray of the elements of a very complex world. Most forms of meditation, say the Tantrists, fly from this disorder into a spuriously simple unity. They are inclined to sacrifice too easily half the truth by trying to force our experience into the other half.

For instance, torn between mind and matter, many meditational systems teach us to regard matter as unreal and to retreat into a "mentalism" that has merely turned its back on the problems associated with the material. Or, uneasy as a relative being, a single, limited person, we are encouraged to forget all relativity in order to imagine ourselves the Absolute. In Buddhist terms, we run away from *samsāra* (the world and all it entails) to *nirvāna* (the condition of utter, transcendent distinctionlessness). Herbert V. Guenther quotes an eminent Tantrist, Saraha, as viewing such attempts with disdain: "By the swindle of meditation freedom is not found."[3]

For Tantra, reality is always perfect but not necessarily still and at rest. Further, it is *at once* both the Absolute and the relative; it is *simultaneously* the indeterminate, undivided, all-embracing One, and this very determinate self I find myself to be. What we must seek, then, is not to forget the finite and know only the infinite, for that would be to falsify reality; we must find a way to unify mind *and* body while taking both seriously, to experience Absoluteness and relativity at once. Whatever we mean by "Reality," it expresses itself as both *nirvāna* and *samsāra*, and both should therefore be honored.

It is this perception that leads Tantra to endorse the use of sexuality as another means toward realization of the truth, for in the fulfillment of orgasm two become one without ceasing to be two. There is here, therefore, a perfect experience of duality within oneness, and this seems to Tantra a better representation of the Truth than any oversimple Monism.

Even for Tantra, however, the goal is the realization of a new perspective and experience achieved by a concentration of our entire psychic and physical being. This achievement loosens us from the illusion that each of us is simply that unsatisfactory "self" we usually think ourselves to be and introduces us to a vision much larger, much safer than our old understanding of ourselves as precariously perched over the terrible abyss of possible destruction.

To be fully collected, supremely whole, and free from the maddening dispersal of thought and feeling is, thus, central to the quest for which most forms of meditation are designed as instruments.

3

God and Meditation

Many of the methods and ideas associated with meditation have no real connection with what most people mean when they use the term "God." It is true that Patanjali's yoga included the act of thinking about and surrendering oneself to God, but this inclusion decisively marked Patanjali off from the Buddhist systems that were taking shape at the same time. Today we find that a great deal of popular meditation is quite indifferent to any concept of deity and certainly has nothing necessarily to do with the doctrines distinctive of Judaism or Christianity.

A question of importance to many persons, then, is whether such a religion as Christianity can be reconciled with that turning inward that seems to dominate schemes of meditation. Is "God" simply another device helping us to concentrate—a kind of mantra, perhaps—or is the Christian's relation with God quite different from the meditator's association with the focus of his or her awareness? Let us examine the practice of some exemplary Christians.

The rules of discipline of some fourth- and fifth-century Christian monks and hermits make it clear that what these believers did to develop their devotion to God was often strikingly similar to the practice of their Hindu or Buddhist counterparts. Mantras—usually single words or short passages from the New Testament or the liturgy—were used to help their concentration; an especially popular one was "Lord, have mercy," or (in its Greek form) *Kyrie eleison.*

Indeed, the evidence we have of the so-called Desert Fathers of

Christendom suggests that their manner of being religious had much more in common with hellenistic or oriental asceticism than with the rather earthy life of the followers of Christ in the Bible. One early source, the *Philokalia*, shows us the ideal meditator as living in solitude in a cell, attempting to suppress thought, and focusing attention by means of what has been called the "Jesus Prayer": "Lord Jesus Christ, Son of God, have mercy upon me, a sinner."[1] This prayer is uttered repeatedly in rhythm with the meditator's breathing until the mind becomes so one-pointed that there is a sense of absolute unity with God.[2]

Saint Ignatius

In the early sixteenth century Saint Ignatius Loyola, an old soldier and disciplinarian turned priest (but still disciplinarian!) devised for his Jesuits a system of "spiritual exercises" that incorporated "every method of examination of conscience, of meditation, of contemplation, of vocal and mental prayer."[3] The method is still in use today among certain Christians (not all of whom are Catholics, let alone Jesuits) and may be considered a very rigorous program intended to achieve striking results fairly quickly. As a matter of fact, one is generally expected to be able to complete the exercises in about thirty days.

In Loyola's method we find the meditators making an effort to purify themselves of all attractions that might seduce them from a wholehearted allegiance to God, and presenting their entire will to God that they might become the instruments of Divine purpose. We have here a very important deviation from many other forms of meditation. It is not the fulfillment or wholeness of the meditator that is here the supreme goal, nor is it the meditator's tranquility or abandoning of ego. All these will be accomplished, but the goal is the fulfillment of the intentions of God for the world.

We find, in this system, the efforts of the faithful being guided by a Director (or Meditation Master and Disciplinarian) who gives instructions for about one week's exercises at a time. To present the complete program at the outset might, it was felt, confuse or discourage the pilgrim, so it was dispensed in small doses.

It would take us too far afield to examine all the elements in this intriguing and demanding approach to enlightened spiritual experience, but it is worth our noticing here that, as in other methods we have considered, there is a close concentrating of attention on objects that are considered helpful in some way. For instance, at certain times the aspirants are told to concentrate on a particular sin that their rigorous examination of their own conscience has unearthed. This is parallel to the contemplation of objectionable features of the body and its functions in Buddhism, both practices being designed, in part, to dispel any illusions about our intrinsic splendor.

Again, one of the methods of prayer used by Loyola consisted of measured, rhythmical recitation:

> With each breath or respiration, one should pray mentally while saying a single word of the *Our Father*, or other prayer. . . . For this same space of time, the attention is chiefly directed to the meaning of the word, to the person who is addressed, to our own lowliness.[4]

The Jesuits were to be the "storm troopers" of a church marching to the beat of God's drum, and Loyola's method of training was thorough, arduous, and psychologically perceptive. Since not all of us are rugged enough to be at the forefront of the continuing war with worldly evil, it is fortunate that the same century brought to the fore other spiritual leaders in Christendom with disciplines no less exacting in the long run, but a little less compressed. One of these was an astonishing woman, Saint Teresa of Avila, among the most highly renowned of Spanish Christian mystics and a contemporary of the illustrious Saint John of the Cross. Her spiritual method contains most of the distinctive features of Christian mysticism.

Saint Teresa

The brilliant but troubled sixteenth century provided the stage on which Teresa played her role. In fact, she was born in the very year in which Martin Luther published his doctrine of salvation by grace through faith. In a small Castilian town named Avila, Teresa de Cepeda y Ahumada, to give her full name, was born into a family that was eventually to consist of twelve children.

As a child, Teresa seems to have been a mixture of piety and frivolity. She had nine brothers with whom she evidently competed in boisterousness while precociously becoming very concerned with her appearance and the impression she was creating. While scarcely more than an infant she devised games sometimes curiously "religious," and with one of her brothers, she actually built little stone "hermitages" around their home, intending to imitate certain solitary saints of whom they had heard. In fact, these two once set out to win heavenly glory for themselves by becoming martyrs! As Teresa herself tells it, "We agreed to go off to the country of the Moors, begging our bread for the love of God, so that they might behead us there. . . . But our greatest hindrance seemed to be that we had a father and a mother."[5]

When she was sixteen, Teresa was placed as a boarding scholar in the Augustinian convent of Our Lady of Grace. She quickly learned to admire the good sisters there, but by no means did she want to become a nun herself. She had never been physically strong, and the change in food and habits here began to undermine her health completely, so that after eighteen months her father was obliged to take her home to Avila. Nevertheless, this period of illness was enormously formative for her. The lingering influence of the gentle sisters, along with the company of a deeply religious and rather austere uncle, helped Teresa to find in her illness a source of thoughtful questions: what is life, this precarious foothold on reality? how is it to be made meaningful?

At last Teresa decided that, despite great misgivings, she must herself become a nun. Although her father resisted this decision, one morning in 1535 she ran away from home. She presented herself as a postulant at the convent and was received. Her father, seeing her determination and realizing the futility of fatherly restraint, reluctantly consented to Teresa's joining the Mitigated Rule of the Order of Mount Carmel.

Throughout Teresa's life—amid her constant battle with illness, her seemingly endless frustrations at the hands of superiors who were horrified at her visions and recommended fatuous disciplines, the skill and courage with which she undertook to reform her Order and expand its activities—her dominant concern was relationship with God, and it was from this center that her observations about purity, discipline, humility, and other virtues emanated. The presuppositions of her theology were few, and they were quite orthodox: God is the Alpha and Omega of all being and, by reason of this infinite majesty and power, God alone finally sets the terms under which any person finds fellowship with the Divine. Indeed, such fellowship is possible at all only because God graciously grants it; our human responsibility is to prepare ourselves for it by penitence, purity of conduct and thought, and ardent, persevering prayer.

It is on the subject of prayer that Teresa is most eloquent; in her writings, prayer and what we have called meditation are intimately related things. True prayer, according to Teresa, has three prerequisites: (1) love of our fellows; (2) detachment from all created things; and (3) true humility.

Speaking first about our love for other people, Teresa complains that we usually have either too much love for each other, or too little. Too much is an evil, because "these intimate friendships are seldom calculated to make for the love of God."[6] She urges, therefore, "For the love of the Lord, refrain from making individual friendships, however holy, for even among brothers and sisters such things are apt to be poisonous."[7]

Instead of close or passionate alliances, Teresa advises a kind of general, equal love for all our fellows, a love without heat, pure and unpossessive. If the object of such love falls into evil ways, he or she is to be gently rebuked, and if the person does not then return to a more reasonable and decent style of life, the friendship with him or her must cease. Thus, Teresa's nuns were to tread a narrow ridge between an excess of affection for their fellows, and a paucity of it. They must above all, she warned, avoid grudges, party strife, pride, and all such disruptive products of unbalanced human relationships.

No less important than love of our fellows is the second of her fundamentals: detachment from all created things. Teresa really meant *all*, including our families, our fondest possessions, the very beauties of the world, and our own will. A suitable detachment includes ridding ourselves of love for our own body and entails only a moderate and reasonable concern about our health.

The point of this rule of detachment is that God should so dominate our concern that no other object, whether within us or around us, can be a rival. We are to be God-centered, with the interests of the Divine Kingdom so much ours also that our will, in effect, becomes like an extension of God's.

Finally, humility is absolutely necessary for the life of effective prayer. Humility is absent not only in clear cases of arrogance or pride, but more subtly in "spiritual" persons who take themselves too seriously. Teresa sometimes speaks about this temptation to be concerned with our own pride and says, "God deliver us from people who wish to serve Him yet who are mindful of their own honour."[8]

Here, then, are the bases upon which a life of prayer is to be built. Of course, they do not stand alone; faith is their foundation. However, it is these three traits—love, detachment, and humility—that Teresa singled out for the special consideration of her nuns.

The Ladder of Prayer

Teresa describes prayer, with its various levels or stages, as a ladder with many steps ascending into the presence of God. At the foot of the ladder is what she calls "vocal prayer." This means the more or less formal speaking of prayers—the Paternoster, Ave Maria, and so on—and Teresa has some critical remarks to make concerning the misuse of these familiar forms: "When people tell you that you are speaking with God by reciting the Paternoster and thinking of worldly things—well, words fail me."[9] It is the thinking of worldly things, not the use of the ancient words, that is offensive, for the attitude of mind and spirit is the thing of primary importance. This remains true, indeed, whether we use some conventional form of prayer or our own spontaneous language:

> . . . The angels in His presence know well that their King is such that He prefers the unskilled language of a humble peasant boy, knowing that he would say more if he had more to say, to the speech of the wisest and most learned men, however elegant may be their arguments, if these are not accompanied by humility.[10]

Vocal prayer, according to Teresa, when it is prayer in the true spirit (and that means with a mind centered firmly on God), is virtually indistinguishable from what is commonly called "mental prayer."

Generally considered a higher form—the next step on the ladder—
mental prayer "consists in thinking of what we are saying, understanding it, and realizing Whom we are addressing, and who we are that are
daring to address so great a Lord."[11]

True prayer begins, therefore, in a fixing of our attention upon
God and the meaning of what we say, and when this happens the door
is open for our advancement into realms utterly beyond our power of
attainment. To those who pray with this degree of earnest sincerity and
concentration God may grant the favor of their being led into the
higher reaches of spiritual adventure. From the point of mental prayer
"it is quite possible for the Lord to grant you perfect contemplation."[12]

The "prayer of contemplation" is the next stage in our spiritual
journey, when it may be said that the divine-human balance in prayer
begins to tilt towards the divine. In this condition,

> Such a person understands that, without any sound of words, she is be-
> ing taught by this Divine Master, Who is suspending her faculties. . . .
> The faculties rejoice without knowing how they rejoice; the soul is en-
> kindled in love without understanding how it loves. . . . It is well aware
> that this is not a joy which can be attained by the understanding. . . . It
> is a gift of the Lord of earth and Heaven.[13]

In "contemplation" we are passive, our attention wholly fixed
and apparently held upon God, while love and joy seem to fill us from
an inexhaustible reservoir which is in no sense our own manufactur-
ing. We seem to be as helpless as a baby, feeding on the nourishment
God offers us, unmoving except as God moves us. This is the threshold
of another stage in prayer, the "prayer of quiet," very near the pinnacle
of mystic experience.

It is clear that in Teresa's view the prayer of quiet is not something that any of us could precipitate. It comes as a gift, and it remains
for as long as God wills that it may. All that we can do is prepare ourselves, make ourselves receptive. If this is done, and yet the great favor
of this kind of prayer is not bestowed, there is no ground for complaint
and there is no point in bewailing its absence. It is, after all, for God to
determine what is good for us, and if God withholds this particular
honor, however earnestly we desire it, it is our part to be reconciled to
Divine purpose and simply to persist faithfully in that level of prayer

which we can attain. For all we know, our perfecting as God's person may be better served by Divine denial of something than by our attaining all that we would wish.

If, however, God does visit us in that special way known as the prayer of quiet, what joy is ours! Teresa's prose rings with exquisite astonishment that God should have granted this high favor to her. Just what is the nature of this level of prayer? "The soul, in a way which has nothing to do with the outward senses, realizes that it is now very close to its God, and that, if it were but a little closer, it would become one with Him."[14] There is a perfect stillness of soul and body and, apparently, a sense that any enforced movement would painfully disturb the rapport with the Divine.

Finally, in this ladder of prayer, comes the experience of union with God. Neither Teresa nor any other mystic has been able to talk with complete coherence about this, or to describe to his or her own satisfaction either the inner nature of the experience, or the spiritual growth and learning which they are all convinced they have derived from it. Often images of marriage are employed to suggest some aspects of the experience. Teresa says,

> But when this most wealthy Spouse desires to enrich and comfort the Bride still more, He draws her so closely to Him that she is like one who swoons from excess of pleasure and joy and seems to be suspended in those Divine arms.[15]

Teresa goes on to say that in this state of prayer one is "wholly absorbed in God's indescribable greatness."[16] Again, "there is no feeling, but only rejoicing, unaccompanied by any understanding of the thing in which the soul is rejoicing."[17] One's sense organs seem to be inoperative; one is simply held perfectly still in ecstasy.

The prayer of union comes only to one who has practiced mental prayer with much perseverance. When it comes, it does not remain for very long at a time—perhaps half an hour at the most—but one learns with experience to remain available to it, and it may recur again and again over a period of several hours.

What actually happens to the subjectivity, the "soul" in traditional language, of the person in a state of union with God? Teresa tells us that while she was pondering this she actually experienced, quite spontaneously, just such a union, and in it Christ Himself answered her question. She seemed to hear Him say, "It dies to itself wholly, daughter, in order that it may fix itself more and more upon Me; it is no longer itself that lives, but I. As it cannot comprehend what it understands, it is an understanding which understands not."[18]

Some of the *effects* of this union are, fortunately, easier to describe than the state itself. There is, Teresa tells us, a new courage, so that "it would be greatly comforted if at that moment, for God's sake, it could be hacked to pieces."[19] New and high resolutions are formed, and there is a gush of fresh vigor to carry them out. But this is accompanied by a new, yet far from depressing or morbid, sense of unworthiness and of God's immeasurable mercy.

Is this, then, the end of the mystic road? Not quite. There is one experience which, in a sense, surpasses even the condition of union so far described, although it is likely to cause some distress and even physical exhaustion—so much so that Teresa "besought the Lord earnestly not to grant me any more favours" of this nature.[20] This additional experience is variously called "elevation," "rapture," "flight of the spirit," or "transport." In it the soul seems to leave the body, perhaps without warning, and one is conscious of being borne upward as on an eagle's wings. Until this has become a familiar adventure it is likely to occasion some alarm, and to Teresa it also presented mild embarrassment because it sometimes happened when she was in public, and the physical—highly visible—manifestations of it were so apparent that although her nuns, at her instruction, held her, others who were present must have been disconcerted by what they noticed, unused as they were in pre-television days to the disarming spectacle of a flying nun.

Saint Teresa's account of her own experience in prayer and concentration contains so many characteristics in common with the vast stream of Christian mysticism that it may serve as a rough generalization. There is, of course, much more to be said even of Teresa. She herself wrote movingly, using analogies that help to make at least something of her experience accessible to most of us. She likened the progress of the soul to such things as the watering of a garden, or as passage through seven mansions, and she frequently drew rather daringly upon nuptial metaphors to convey something of her meaning.

In what ways does Teresa's experience coincide with the meditational discoveries we have already examined? Clearly the central facets we found there are also here. In Teresa's prayer there is an increasing measure of concentration, using prayers (sometimes the brief, ritualized prayers familiar to church liturgies) as vehicles of this effort. The "Lord's Prayer" or Paternoster becomes, in some respects, rather like an extended mantra, and the mind is ever more narrowly and completely brought to bear on its object.

Again, we discover once more here the experience of being absorbed, by degrees, until the self-conscious self is gone in an ecstatic condition of unity with the All. There is also a concern for purity, which most meditational systems regard as an essential prerequisite of success; there is an appreciation of humility, and there is a discipline which is, in some ways, an echo of the other systems. The notes, familiar to us now, of detachment from persons and things in conjunction with a sort of universal compassion, are clearly sounded, and Teresa's long and careful self-scrutinies, leading to acts of confession, are not unlike the "Mindfulness" of Buddhist disciplines.

We are, then, on familiar ground in much of what Teresa tells us. Yet there is something new in her writing, too. Teresa is convinced that all *we* can accomplish is a natural condition of mind (or "soul" if we may permit her the word) which is less than the actual union with God. The ultimate condition of the mystic is simply not something he or she can generate by any amount or kind of discipline; it is a gift, a "coming" of the Divine who is free from us and not to be manipulated by our self-manipulations. We can present ourselves in readiness for a Divine visit, but we cannot make God come. God is immeasurably more than even our most perfect state of consciousness.

Teresa, as we have seen, sometimes resorted to nuptial, even to sexual metaphor. If she had continued in that vein to discuss true and false mystical or meditative attainment she might have said that the soul's authentic union with the true God Who is both its life and yet its eternal Other was like marriage. In contrast, the attainment of a sense of unity which was no more than a turning inward into oneself, a modification of one's own consciousness, was rather like—to use a simile that Teresa herself certainly would not have chosen—spiritual masturbation.

In any case, the most important new note here is that it is essential to let God be God, and to wait patiently. This is a theistic theme that recurs in the precepts of other meditators who look beyond the "zero" of nondifferentiating awareness to the living Ground, as they conceive God, of all that is.

It is a pity that the European mystical tradition is so little known by most of us today, for it contained some astonishing and colorful characters and some remarkable accomplishments. The delightful variety of unique personalities presented to us from this source can only be suggested by the mention of such persons as Saint Augustine, Dionysius, Saint John of the Cross, Saint Bernard, Bunyan, Lawrence, Saint Francis, Tauler, Von Hugel, Donne, Eckhart, Boehme, Fox, and Underhill. If we extend our inventory to include Jewish and Muslim members, the list becomes endless. Amid this variety there are some reasonably consistent strands of thought and experience that may help us, as Teresa has done, to think about the connections and disconnections between theistic mysticism and the largely non-theistic meditation we have discussed.

Typical of the long Christian tradition and, I think, also of theistic traditions in general, is the sense that the mystical pilgrimage passes through three broad stages. First there is what some have called the "Purgative" life, consisting of self-examination, contrition, confession, attempts to amend what has been wrong in one's manner of thinking and behaving—in short, coming to terms with what one is and deliberately striving for purity of mind and conduct. This is always felt to be essential to a really sound outcome of whatever other spiritual disciplines may be in use.

Second, the Western mystic embraces the "Illuminative" life, or the life devoted to concentration of mind and will upon God. Many methods may be used here—words or prayers are sometimes virtually employed as mantras, or the symbols of the Faith are used as mandalas; the technique of Brother Lawrence was merely a sensitivity to the pervasive presence of the Divine everywhere and in everything. In any case, concentration, focused attention, is the primary characteristic of this phase.

Third, there is the so-called "Unitive" life—the experience of immediately knowing God either in union, in which one's own center of awareness seems to vanish and be replaced by the Divine, or in communion, in which the mystic and God are together in an ineffable intimacy that, while completely absorbing the energies, devotion, and in some sense awareness of the mystic, does not dissolve that person's existence as a separate consciousness.

Conclusion

The wholeness sought in meditation is often experienced as a new or altered consciousness. This means, in some cases, such concentration of mind that the meditator seems at last to merge with the meditation object or with the process of meditation itself, until there is a state like contentless consciousness in which, and after which, old clingings to certain loyalties, commitments, assumptions, and other contents of the old self-consciousness drop away. The subjects feel they have transcended whatever disturbed, confined, or threatened them, and they enjoy a new unity not only of consciousness but, they are convinced, of being. They may look at the world of multiplicity and even enjoy playing in it, but they do so now from a center which simultaneously observes that shadow world of things, and yet exists on a higher plane, above worldly distinctions, unthreatenable.

In some cases, "mindful" observation of one's own mental, emotional, and physical operations leads at last to the dismissal of these as ephemeral and "not I" and then to the delightful sense of flowing with the general movement of things, free of any ego to afflict concern, any self to be protected—simply at one with all that is.

Among the devout who meditate in the faith that God is the Supreme Reality, there may come the experience of an altered state in which one knows blissful unity or joyous community with this God.

But whatever the precise shape of the ultimate state of awareness (or state beyond awareness) may be, it is certainly intended that it will increasingly permeate all one's other states of mind, so that living in the routine world of affairs will itself come to be transformed by the perceptions gained and the lingering influence of what one has presumed to be a "higher" sensitivity.

Certainly, then, there are states of consciousness different from that in which we generally spend our waking time, but how shall we confirm or disconfirm the meditator's conviction that these states are valuable? This question must be considered carefully.

A further question, and surely an important one, is whether the God of the mystic is no more than the wholeness experienced by the non-theist counterparts. Are we dealing in every case with an experience that is identical, in all important respects, from one subject to another regardless of conflicting philosophical or theological assumptions?

And what about the sense of "truth" that successful meditators attribute to their most intense experiences? Have those anything to do with "reality" beyond the meditators themselves, or are all altered states merely that—altered conditions of the psyche with no further significance? Do they, perhaps, tell us more about the needs, fears, and insecurities a person has fled, and the delusions that are able to comfort him or her, than about Reality?

There are many questions that no amount of bold assertion, charismatic insistence, or cheap one-upmanship ("I've *had* the experience; obviously you haven't, so there's nothing you can understand about it") can settle.

4

What Seems to Be Happening?

Many scholars have examined the psychological and physiological effects of meditation. In order to understand our subject and evaluate certain claims made for certain altered states of consciousness, we must consider what secular, scientific investigation can tell us about what happens to a person who is meditating.

Psychoanalysis

Since the pioneering work of Freud, a number of his followers have studied altered states of consciousness. Freud himself, in a lucid but controversial little book entitled *Civilization and Its Discontents*,[1] took note of the familiar mystical or meditative feeling of a "oneness" in which the individuality of the person meditating was dissolved in a sense of the complete unity of all things. He wondered what this really signified, since the person having it was patently still that human being whom Freud could see as unalterably separate from Freud himself and from everything and everyone else. He tried to imagine what this sense of "universal oneness" must be like, and concluded that it bore striking resemblance to the bland and blank "awareness" that one may presume a newborn baby to have.

Within the womb, we suppose, the embryo has no sense of a world divided into particular things; it makes no distinction between "myself" and "others." Even when it is first born the baby may still, at first, be innocent of any awareness of differences. In other words, the embryo's, and perhaps the baby's, mental life must be rather featureless—like a vast, uninterrupted sea. Experience with the world, the actual encounter with things other than itself, awakens the baby to the difference between itself and others.

If this is true, if life itself in a world of many objects breaks our consciousness open to the fact of "otherness" and gives us the power to begin to discriminate between this and that, may it not be that the mystic's "oceanic feeling" (as Freud called it) of complete unity with all is a regression, a turning back, to our state of mind before we were born? Is mysticism, then, or meditative "oneness," no more than a false, psychological "return to the womb" and a rejection of the discomfortingly alien character of the real world?

As he thought about this and talked with more of his patients, Freud speculated that some people retain a kind of "memory trace" of that early state of undisturbed and blank consciousness, and that they are more adept than most of us at bringing the condition to the surface. Such people, he suggested, are the potential mystics among us. All they need is an effective method of awakening the embryonic "memory" and entering into it thoroughly.

This is an explanation that is not necessarily pleasing to the mystic, and Freud did not intend that it should be. It seems to reduce an allegedly sublime experience to a retreat that has no more significance than a short vacation from reality.

Another investigator, F. Alexander, after a close study of Buddhist methods of training, described their effect in Freudian terms. He raised the possibility that although Buddhists are fond of saying that they are eliminating their "ego" they may, in fact, be doing nothing of the sort. They are using a term made familiar by Freud ("ego") without Freud's meaning, and this may help them to mistake the actual goal they reach. It is *not* the destruction of the ego that they experience, but the redirection of *libido*.

In other words, Alexander is suggesting that the Buddhists he observed were engaged in withdrawing their psychic energy from the world about them and reinvesting all of it in the ego (their own subjectivity) itself. All their efforts to eliminate desire, to become detached from things, to forsake involvement in whatever they had formerly valued, resulted in the turning of their energies inward so completely that they were at last pure, energized ego, aloof from the challenge of other realities. There is certainly a sense of wholeness to be gained in this way, and those who practice it are likely to have dissolved all boundaries and transcended all limits of thought, but instead of a wholesome selflessness they have actually reached a state of narcissism (or preoccupation with some aspect of their own subjectivity) so complete that they spuriously disvalue every distinction the real world would present to them.[2]

Here again we have an explanation of meditative experience that will not please some, but that deserves to be pursued because it makes sense of many things. A theory is not discredited because we do not like it, nor is it vindicated if we do. We must be prepared to take seriously every promising line of inquiry.

James H. Leuba was another influential observer of mysticism, and it is worth noting that as early as 1912 he was discussing similarities between the reports of mystics and those of certain drug users. His subjects were almost exclusively theists (believers in God), and Leuba found their experience of contact with God to be something they had woven out of some of their own needs and misconceptions. "In seeking intercourse with God in the disappearance of diversity . . . in a sense of freedom and illumination," he wrote, "the mystics have followed a wrong way."[3]

But why is the mystic way "wrong"? Here Leuba does not seem to go beyond Freud. He assumes that the development of logical, rational, linear thought is the highest achievement of humankind, an attainment reached only after millennia of painful evolution out of a primitive condition in which our consciousness was as undifferentiated as the newborn baby's still is, and as the mystic's comes to be. We ought to regard clear, discriminating thought as the proper direction for courageous and meaningful human development. Its rejection in favor of the more intuitive and non-separating state of mind favored by mystics is a reversal of the direction of evolution, a failure to be worthy of the struggling heritage of our kind. To see and think clearly and to make accurate distinctions between different real objects is sometimes hard and may cause anxiety; but it is the way forward for our species, the way to a truly "higher" intelligence.

We are concerned here only with a typical sample of a genre, and what we have seen is fairly standard for psychoanalytic investigations. Even Carl G. Jung, whose thought often seems superficially to be more friendly to the kind of experience we are discussing, really reduces its significance by the limited function his Individual Psychology allows it.[4] The work of all these psychologists probably makes an important contribution to our grasp of what meditation achieves, but we must not remain content with it, partly because so much of it is not exactly science but the fruit of a keen distaste for what they were studying. Their line of investigation will continue, and they have provided questions that must be taken seriously, especially the question of whether the most "advanced" states of meditative consciousness are or are not "higher" or more valuable than ordinary thought, and whether they might not instead be flights from reality.

Psycho-physiology

We now approach an area that may be a little more difficult for the uninitiated to follow, but that promises to be worth the effort. Recently there have evolved some new methods of study for our subject, making use of equipment and concepts unimagined by earlier researchers. These methods offer a new and different set of suggestions about what meditation accomplishes for us.

First we should remind ourselves that meditation uses an array of methods. Sometimes the results of different techniques may themselves be different, and when this is found to be the case we may have gained a new clue about what meditation actually does in us. Many Indian yogins, for example, work to eliminate from their awareness all sensory experience, retreating from the world and not using any part of their senses even as a focus for concentration. They strive not simply to close their minds to anything outside, but to seal them shut. On the other hand, certain meditators are willing to become sharply "mindful" of things presented to them by their senses, but they so focus their attention that intensity and concentration are achieved.

Again, some meditation systems try to pacify the body and make the mind perfectly still, while others, such as Kundalini Yoga, try to stimulate a smooth flow of energy by their concentration of attention. It would be a mistake to assume, as some earlier scholars did, that the psychological and physiological effects of such different procedures would be quite identical. So we may ask, in what ways do different major methods of meditation have different effects within us?

Widely reported tests of Indian yogins by Bagchi and Wenger in 1957, and by Anand, Chhina, and Sing in 1961, showed that when meditating deeply these subjects produced EEG (electroencephalogram) patterns that were dominated by "alpha waves," the kind of brain "wave" or energy pattern that is mainly associated with relaxation—the kind we all tend to produce when sleeping deeply and without dreams. When a sudden noise or some other outside stimulus was introduced, the yogins automatically ignored it—their EEG showed no response at all and their restful alpha waves flowed on.

The point is not that these meditators were asleep, but that they had achieved a condition of perfect relaxation and had learned to resist its interruption.

By contrast, Kasamatsu and Hirai in 1966 examined some Zen masters and discovered an intriguingly different state of affairs. They, too, had EEG patterns dominated by alpha waves, but this pattern changed abruptly and briefly every time a new stimulus was presented—that is, every time a sharp click was made to occur. Nor did these Zen adepts ever become so used to this intrusive stimulus that their alert response to it diminished. Whenever it occurred there was a momentary break in the flow of alpha waves.

Like the yogins in India, the Japanese Zen masters had achieved the ability to empty their minds of content, but their method of doing so had left them closer to the world and more accessible to it. This does not mean that their meditative achievement was inferior, but simply that it was different. In both cases meditation brought relaxation, but in the one there remained a capacity to respond to the world outside consciousness, and in the other that world had virtually ceased to exist.

Two other investigators, Das and Gastaut, studied Kundalini Yoga in 1957 and found yet another result. The Tantric meditators they examined did not produce significant alpha waves at all. Rather, there were dominant "beta" rhythms recorded from them, rhythms that indicate a state of activity or excitation. Now, these people had been busy in the attempt to arouse "Kundalini," the dormant energy at the base of the spine, and to urge this to follow its proper circuitry through-out the body. Their minds, too, were perfectly concentrated but were in quite a different state, a more active one, than were the minds of the yogins and Zenists.[5]

It begins to appear, from this, that even when similar words are used to describe the final experience of meditation ("insight," "enlight-enment," "true seeing," and the rest), the method of meditating shapes significantly the actual physiological results obtained. This raises the question of whether there is, after all, a single kind of "truth" to be reached by meditation, or whether instead what we do determines what we find, and one kind of "enlightenment" may actually question the final truth of another.

Indeed, we are faced with an even more serious question. The manipulation of consciousness through meditation appears to be also the manipulation of our body, and the question (to which we must re-turn) cannot be avoided: is it anything more than that?

Biofeedback

To see more clearly the possible connection between control of the body and control of the mind, we may make a brief excursion into a very modern medical development, the technique called "biofeed-back training"—surely one of the most repulsive names ever foisted on an interesting subject.

The procedure here is to connect a person to an electronic monitoring device that detects, amplifies, and registers changes in some selected physical process within the subject's body. There are sev-eral uses of this technique, but the one that interests us at present is the deliberate cultivation of alpha waves in the activity of the brain. This is used to help someone who suffers from hypertension to deliberately "calm down."

It has been shown to be possible for persons to control their own production of alpha rhythms if they are kept informed, by the device, of the brain's electrical activity. Patients who had formerly been heavily sedated in order to become calm have learned quickly to manufacture restful alpha waves. After studying the data, Ralph Ezios remarks that it would seem that with very little training and the aid of a "feedback" machine, any normal person could learn to achieve a state of mind similar to that of a Zen monk or a yogin.[6]

What does this suggest for the significance of meditation? It begins to appear that, whatever interpretation one may prefer to give them, the actual events that occur in the human being as a result of meditation are simple matters of the control of electrochemical functions. Meditation seems to be a way of regulating the electrical impulses of the nervous system.

The effects of this control may, of course, be interpreted by the meditator according to some idea or some symbol system he or she accepts (that is, some philosophical or religious system of belief); but whatever the beliefs, the actual organic event is a modification of electrical performance.

To put this bluntly, it can be argued that one does not need Advaita, Buddhist, Christian, or any other particular philosophy to attain what is achieved organically in meditation. These symbol systems may provide a rich interpretive framework, and at least one of them may even be valid, but the bodily result is not dependent on any of them.

However, the achievement of tranquility and rest is not the only reported result of meditation. Some meditators, for instance, extol the sense of liberation from the old "self" with its weight of confusion, guilt, and anxiety. Do studies of physiological psychology throw any light on this result?

Losing the "Self" and Dropping Habits

Many persons, in various religious traditions, have reported that at a certain stage in their meditation they reached a point where consciousness became "pure"—no longer the consciousness of something, but just consciousness. For a seemingly timeless moment all was perfectly still, with no movement of ideas, impressions, or feelings. When this moment was ended, the persons having it were aware of being "free" from things that had formerly imprisoned them; they seemed to have stepped back from themselves and to have realized that what they thought themselves to be was spurious. The cluster of emotions and ideas, of taste and distaste with which they had identified themselves is seen to be quite detachable, a sort of casing that they had allowed to enclose them. The old identity, the old "self" is seen as a fabrication, a shabby coat, and not what they really are at all. What they *are* is the pure consciousness that has escaped. Can we find the physiological or psychological basis of this experience, and will it help to interpret the experience itself?

Robert Ornstein has written, "It seems that a consequence of the structure of our central nervous system is that if awareness is restricted to one unchanging source of stimulation, a 'turning off' of consciousness of the external world follows."[7] This means that when attention is held still, concentrated on some single object, for even a short time, with absolutely no wavering or the intrusion of other objects, ideas, or images, a sort of "blink" occurs in which consciousness actually tunes out even that one object on which it was focused. The result is that the subject is very briefly quite conscious but without any content in his or her consciousness.

It does not matter, by the way, what the object of our concentrated attention is; we might use anything, so long as the mind is being held steady, and experiments have shown that a *ganzfeld* (a plain, white surface) will serve as well as anything else.

Curiously, yet quite naturally, after this "blink" the subjects are usually a little detached from their former mental furniture. They feel as if they had stepped out of a set of self-understandings, as if they had put off a mask.

What does this experience mean? Meditative traditions tell us that what is left after we have thrown off the encrusting self-image is our true "self," our actuality. We have "dropped the ego" and become, perhaps, Reality itself, without boundaries or limits. Can this be so, or does science offer us another way of seeing the matter? For an answer to this we must turn to some recent studies of the phenomena called "habituation" and "dehabituation."

Habituation and Becoming a Self

A great deal of our behavior is a matter of habit. We do not stop every moment to ask ourselves, "What shall I do about that?" On the contrary, we learn while we are still small children that some common situations can safely be handled with the same behavior every time they arise, and the result is that this behavior becomes automatic—we simply do it without thinking about it. When we return home late at night and find our house in darkness, we do not wonder what to do. Unlocking the door and then switching on lights as we go are such familiar procedures that we do them by habit. Many of our regular actions and even our beliefs are like this: they are habits of response, and we have long since given up thinking about them.

How do we form such habits? Some theorists believe that an infant forms its first set of automatic responses to the world even before it learns to speak or to think in words. That is to say, it develops a kind of pre-verbal understanding of a few experiences such as comfort, fear, and maybe loss, and it learns ways of behaving that bring comfort and avoid the other two emotions. "Habituation" or learning to do spontaneously things that seem to be appropriate may, then, be one of our first accomplishments.

As we learn to speak, however, a new stage begins in our struggle to cope with the world. Evidence suggests that the infant does not take his or her old pre-verbal understandings and carefully apply the new words to them (as if it said, "Comfort: ah yes, that's the word for that dear old experience of lying on soft pillows"); rather, the child seems to re-learn the meaning of his or her experience. The new verbal understanding actually overlays and suppresses the former inarticulate one. So we learn for the second time how to live in the world and get what we want from it, but language has now become the chief tool for recognizing our experiences and shaping behavior that seems suitable for them.

Why is language so valuable that it can overlay the older kind of understanding and drive it from memory? Partly, no doubt, because it makes our thinking more systematic and allows us to consider options and invent a range of possible responses. It enables us to reflect before acting, to experiment in our mind with alternative behaviors before committing ourselves to one of them, and to be more critical of behaviors that may not have worked very well.

Language, then, is a way by which we gradually shape our understanding of the world and our response to it, and it is more effective than the first, pre-verbal one. It helps us, at last, to build up a repertoire of behaviors that have been found to work, and the time comes when a very large part of our daily activity is formed by this accumulated experience so that we act from habit rather than from continuing reflection and decision.

Already we can see one possible explanation of the effect of the "blink" that meditation sometimes brings to our consciousness. It may be a stepping back behind our verbalized understandings into the frame of mind in which pre-verbal (or, as we are inclined to say, "intuitive") understandings operate. It is often felt to be liberating, to make us more capable of spontaneity, because the set of habits that developed out of years of verbal thinking has become rigid and confining. But we must press our explanation further than this if even this point is to become clear.

One of the tasks we give to language and verbal thinking is that of making the world intelligible and safe. We want to understand what is happening and what is likely to happen, and words are the means by which we put together our interpretation of events and things. In time our explanations become so much a part of our system of habits that they are as automatic as breathing, and we "see" the world around us by means of them. In other words, we often do not see the world or persons in it as they really are, but as our habits of understanding and interpretation present them to us. We see the world only after it has been edited by habits of thought. We notice only what fits into our accepted, habitual way of understanding things. This may make us feel comfortable and "at home" in the world we see, but it may also mean that a great deal of that world escapes our attention.

Occasionally we are forced to notice our unconscious editing of our world. A friend, perhaps even a spouse whom we have lived with for decades, does something that seems out of character and we are surprised—even shocked. We immediately think, "This person has changed!" But it may not be that he or she has changed at all; it may be that we have seen the person only in the limited terms of our habitual response to him or her, we have not seen all that the person is. The present behavior is not inconsistent with what the person is, but only with what we have thought him or her to be. Startled out of our habit of perceiving, we may begin to pay attention to such persons again and (until habit takes over once more) to see them as they are.

Now, among our habits of interpretation may be found certain values. What is "good" and what is "bad"? Out of experience we reach some answer to this question and, after we do, our ideas of the good and bad in life tend to be no longer questioned but become the unexamined premises on which we judge and automatically respond to everything and everyone around us. We "like" one person and reject another not because of careful reflection, but because habits of perceiving what is good or bad automatically shape our feelings.

In summary, each of us tends, very early in life, to become a complex set of habits: habits of valuing, acting, noticing, and thinking about ourselves, of "imaging" ourselves in a consistent way. We "know who we are" because the image we have constructed fits our particular set of values, assumptions, and experiences. It is, indeed, woven out of them.

When we speak about our "mind" or our "character" we are really pointing to a set of habits. And when we talk about "the world," we really mean that model of the world which we have created out of habits of perceiving and judging.

Our models of the world and of ourselves may, in fact, be reasonably accurate, but they are inevitably limited and therefore confining. We drift along, rarely, if ever, noticing things that are inconsistent with the models, and for this reason, as we grow older we enjoy fewer and fewer surprises. The delight of wonder is gone and the sense of mystery has perished. If our model is too narrow, we find at last with Hamlet that the world is "weary, stale, flat and unprofitable" and we are bored. We have allowed ourselves to become bundles of habit whose images of reality are our prisons.

But suppose something happens to detach us from the models? Ah, then the world outside us, and even we ourselves, may be seen more accurately. We become new once again in a new world.

This, I believe, is part of what may happen when meditation brings our central nervous system to the moment of "blink," the moment when consciousness empties itself and, as if purified, returns to the world loosened from its old habits of perception and response.

Our awareness has been the prisoner of habit for a long time;

then there is a moment when awareness steps out of the prison. It becomes "bare awareness" without the shelter of its old conventions. It sees the world, and ourselves, with a feeling that walls have tumbled down. It does not simply experience itself as free, but as more real, more authentic than before. And since the old habits were what we thought of as our "self," we are now without self.

There is danger in this. If this experience occurs without adequate preparation, the moment of dehabituation may not, after all, be experienced as liberation but as loss; we may feel confused and estranged from reality. We may be disoriented—"beside ourselves" as the common phrase has it.

Fortunately, most systems of meditation are embedded in a philosophy that is thoroughly familiar to the meditator. A new set of habits of perception and interpretation is already in place to take over from the old ones; but since this is a *new* set, it is not felt as confining, and even though it also functions to limit and interpret what the meditator can understand, its very newness prevents it from being boring, and the person slips into it with only a sense of escape from the old.

The difference between being merely rid of an old system of habits and being immediately transformed by a new set is charmingly illustrated by the familiar story attributed to Jesus in Luke 11:24–26. Using the conceptions of his time, Jesus tells of a man from whom an unclean or unwholesome "spirit" has been driven out but who, as a result, becomes simply vacant (as we would say, with no system of interpretation). In time the old spirit, plus an assortment of others that are equally unsatisfactory, fill this void and the man is in worse turmoil than before. We may say that the man had been set free of old habits, an old model of world and self, but since there was no new model prepared for him, he not only relapsed at last into his well-worn modes of thinking, but actually became the victim of ill-considered ideas and ways of viewing things. Nature, it is said, abhors a vacuum, and this is as true of our selfhood as of anything else. If we achieve the meditative "blink" that loosens old custom, we will be fortunate if a new philosophy is ready for instant adoption.

However, the world is full of such systems, ready made for our adoption. Buddhism, Vedanta, Islam, Christianity, Judaism, Materialism, Humanism, Rationalism, Marxism, Romanticism, Idealism—

there is an almost endless list of those great systems of meaning and conviction that have provided the materials for the new "free" being who has shuffled off the old confining "self" in meditation. Which of them we choose after our "blink" usually depends not on careful critical evaluation, but on which of them has been constructing itself or its assumptions at some level of our mind before the blink occurs. Whichever system it is, however, it will seem to us self-evidently true and irreproachably profound.

This may be a rather disconcerting view of things. Among other possibilities, it raises the point that no (absolutely *no*) system of meaning is proven by our having experienced an awakening to it. We shall, however, leave this for the moment.

One interpretation of successful meditation, then, is as a process of *de*habituation that may be followed by a *re*habituation. Much that we experience in meditation may be plausibly explained in this way, but there is a wide range of remarkable experiences that meditators report (other than loss of the old "self" and the gaining of a new perspective). Can our hypothesis of dehabituation account for more?

Arthur J. Deikman has developed a hypothesis similar in many ways to the one above, but goes on to ask whether it can ask a wider set of questions. Can such a way of understanding the nature and function of meditative experience account for the meditator's summit experiences of (a) intense reality, (b) strikingly unfamiliar sensations, (c) unity, (d) ineffability, and (e) trans-sensate phenomena?

Intensification of Reality

It is often reported that some altered states of consciousness are extraordinarily vivid and carry with them the sense of being disclosures of something more "real" than the world of our ordinary perception. However, Deikman argues that a sense of "realness" is not convincing evidence that the world is actually being seen more accurately. There are many clinical examples of variability in the intensity of the feeling of realness that are not to be correlated with actual variability of the reality being perceived.[8] In other words, the feeling of realness is quite different from an accurate judgment of it. As Deikman says, "Realness can be considered a quantity function capable of displacement and, therefore, of intensification, reduction, and transfer" from one mental object to another.[9] We may be mistaken in thinking that our new understanding is more realistic than its predecessor.

Deikman suggests that as the meditator withdraws his attention from external objects and breaks the hold of habitual responses, the feeling of reality that formerly attached to those objects may attach itself instead to something that is entirely *within the mind*, so that thoughts, images, or simply awareness itself "becomes real" to us with a new intensity; a mental condition may thus seem to have more reality than the world around us.[10] This means that the sense of being cosmic, without limits, of being God, Reality, Brahman, and so on, may seem far more real than the world outside us because we have transferred to this state of mind some or all of the feeling of realness that we had formerly divided among the objects of the world. Dropping the old "habit" of attributing realness to things in our environment may make possible an intensified attributing of it to something within us.

Unfamiliar Sensations

Among the things that may lead us to trust unusual states of mind are extraordinary sensory, or pseudo-sensory, experiences such as floods of light, an almost tangible peace, a rush of energy, marvelous but incommunicable knowing, and visions. These may strengthen our belief that we are discovering a truth or finding reality. Can a theory of dehabituation suggest the mechanism by which these happen?

Deikman suggests that all these "sensory" wonders may be understood as the products not of an unusual perception but of an unusual *mode* of perceiving. They may arise naturally out of a change in the way our attention is focused.

It is not difficult to see how tranquility and joy may come to us in the moment when some deeply rooted conflict has been resolved by our abandoning of some rigid value or belief, but how can we explain the seeming sensations of great light and flowing energy?

Deikman's investigations suggest that the sense of energy or force may be the result of our becoming aware of something within us that we formerly ignored because we were habituated to it. That is, as we are loosened from preoccupation with our familiar range of objects, our attention "picks up" subjective data which, until now, it had ignored (or had ignored since we were infants). We had become habituated to the exchange of energy within us and thus had failed to notice it, just as a railway worker may fail to hear the roar of an oncoming train. When our pattern of habituation is broken, suddenly we become aware of things that we had overlooked, including the flow and surge of our own energy.

As for the experience of light, Deikman believes that this may be the human organism's way of experiencing the sudden flood of energy that is released when our concentration is unified and all conflict in awareness is expelled. Light, like the feeling of force, may simply be the way our nervous system registers our moment of dehabituation.

In support of this theory, Deikman says that these extraordinary experiences and visions are most likely to occur when our attention is shifted from the usual set of objects to the process of attending itself, and, further, when analytic thought is suspended and we are not being critical but are willing to receive any stimulus at all, quite unselectively. These are conditions that meditation is likely to produce, but not meditation alone. The same set of conditions can occur in any moment when our attention is focused on our own perceiving or experiencing. Marghanita Laski seems to confirm this view when she reports that mystical experiences like those we are discussing have occurred quite spontaneously in persons undergoing childbirth, viewing landscapes, listening to music, or enjoying sexual intercourse.[11]

All this amounts to the theory that in certain conditions a person may become aware not of things and events outside him or her, but of inner or intra-psychic processes. Dehabituation—the breaking of our usual way of attending to things—is the trigger; and bursts of light, wonderful peace, surges of energy, a sense of knowing something that cannot be said, and even indescribable visions are merely the effects of this change of focus, as natural as the feeling of pain when a nerve in our tooth becomes diseased, and perhaps no more significant for the meaning of life.

Unity

We have seen that Freud and others interpreted the sense of unity with all reality (Freud's "oceanic feeling" or the sense that "all is One") as a kind of mental return to the womb. Deikman concedes that it may, on the contrary, be a perception of the real nature of reality, or it may be no more than the perception of one's own psychic being when all objective and external stimuli have been removed and one is attending only to one's own inwardness.

When we are having an experience of something out there in the world, it is obviously not that actual "something" that enters our brain. Rather, the event that is happening within us is an electrochemical one, an activity of our central nervous system whose product is a perception or an idea. In other words, while we may have many ideas, the "substance" of them, so far as our brain is concerned, is always the same: electrochemical activity. If all outside objects are removed from our attention, and awareness is, so to speak, turned in upon itself, we may experience the unity of our brain activity as if we were perceiving a universal oneness (attributing what is inside us to what is outside us). To put this simply, we may experience the oneness of our experiencing process and mistake it for a oneness in the universe.[12] Once again dehabituation—ceasing to attend to outside things and concentrating on awareness itself—may be the cause of a possibly mistaken understanding.

Ineffability

Some of the meditator's experiences are said to be ineffable— that is, they overwhelm or escape our power of description. Sometimes even more common experiences are like this. "Words fail me!" is a cliché we (like Saint Teresa) utter when our moral feelings are so outraged that no possible combination of words could do justice to our experience.

Let us remember that, according to one theory, many of our earliest childhood experiences are lost to memory not only because they were intense (at a time when we had little experience to encourage the diversification of our attention), but because they occurred before we had any words with which to name and interpret them. These, too, were "ineffable." It is arguable, then, that some of our altered states of consciousness may be ineffable because, through the loss of our conventionalized and verbal ways of habitual noticing, we have spontaneously recovered the memory or pre-verbal experience. Deikman says, for example, that the mystic's occasional sense of being "ineffably" enfolded in love may be the recovery of our infantile experience at the mother's breast. The equally "ineffable" sense of unity with All may be a recovered recollection of our experience as an embryo!

If this is so, many altered states are to be understood as the result when layers of verbalized, habituated experience are suddenly stripped away. We then reach a memory that becomes our experience of the moment, and is as ineffable as it originally was. This is not exactly a return to the womb, but at least it is a return to a very early stage of mental development.

But in addition to this sort of explanation, Deikman offers the view that some quite sudden understandings may be too complex for successful verbalization. If one felt that he had seen, all at once, a total explanation of the working of the entire universe, it would surely be such a multi-faceted vision that he would not know where to begin speaking about it. Such complex understandings (or even misunderstandings) may well occur.

Trans-sensate Phenomena

Some meditators report an experience that "does not include feelings of warmth, sweetness, visions, or any other elements of familiar sensory or intellectual experience."[13] They say that what they enjoyed was quite beyond ordinary ideas, memories, or pathways. Their awareness was by no means vacant, but utterly *different*. This is what we mean by "trans-sensate" phenomena.

Deikman deals with this by saying that when dehabituation releases our attention from its usual objects and ways of editing them, we may become aware of other parts of what he calls the "stimulus array"—that is, the range of objects about us and within us that had been ignored before. Imagine a person whose hearing had been limited to a very narrow range of sound (say he or she could hear only B flat) and who, by a successful bit of surgery, suddenly acquired a fully human spectrum of receptivity. All at once the person could hear Mozart! He or she would certainly feel that this new experience was utterly beyond the old and beyond any words that might have described it.

As we have seen, it is likely that our usual experiencing (and therefore our idea of what can be experienced) is severely limited by habituation. Actually there may be a much greater richness in the objects around us than we realize and a much wider range of things to attend to within us than we guessed. To be set free from the old editings, then, leaves us open to notice new things and thus to be sensitive to impressions that are outside our former set. This is not to say that what we now experience is supernatural, or even that our new perceiving is more accurate than the old except in the sense that it is more inclusive. Indeed, we may be so awed by the new impressions that we overrate them and falsely disvalue the familiar. But if we can judiciously and wisely integrate the new and the old, we have a richer and more diverse experience.

In the work of Arthur Deikman we have seen, then, an attempt to make sense of the remarkable effects of meditation through the concept of dehabituation. To do this does not in the least trivialize our fresh awareness, but it does make it possible to put it in perspective and realize that meditative awareness is perfectly human awareness and may not give us any understanding that is necessarily superior or less fallible than others.

Bimodal Consciousness and Split Brain Theories

Other recent research seems to indicate that either the brain itself or its product, thought, is divided between two different functions, one of which tends to become dominant. If any such theory is true (and we leave that for further research), we may have yet another way of explaining some of the effects of meditation.

Deikman, with his concept of "bimodal consciousness,"[14] tells us that our human organisms are designed to react to the world in two main ways: action and reception. Both are necessary, but one may capture our attention and most of our energy.

Obviously we are beings who must act upon our environment. To survive we must deal realistically with the world around us, taking food from it, protecting ourselves from its hazards, finding comfort and shelter in it. All this is part of what Deikman and others mean by the "action mode" of our being. The striate muscle system, in conjunction with the sympathetic nervous system, is the chief physiological agent of this activity.

When we are operating actively, trying to deal effectively with the environment, reaching out to use it or change it or achieve some goal within it, our baseline muscle tension increases, and an EEG would register increased beta waves. In this active state we are inclined to be fairly well focused in our attention, clearly aware of the relevant objects around us and their shapes, and we tend to be interested in seeing not merely things but uses of things. We are likely to be thinking logically and to be more sensitive to shapes than to colors or textures, unless these are important for designing our action.

In short, when we are mobilized for action our perceiving is acute regarding shape, and our thinking is fairly orderly and clear. As Deikman puts it, "Sharp perceptual boundaries are matched by sharp conceptual boundaries, for success in acting on the world requires a clear sense of self-object difference."[15]

Our other main form of operation is the *receptive,* and in this we are devoted not to acting on the environment but simply to taking it in or being aware of it. Here the physiological instruments most in use are the sensory-perceptual system, instead of the muscles, and the parasympathetic nervous system. An EEG might reveal the presence of relaxing alpha waves rather than beta, and our attention inclines to be less narrowly focused, less inclined to detect differences, while our thinking may not be particularly orderly. This is a mode of being that seems to dominate us more often in infancy than later when the very need to survive becomes more acute.

It is always easier for us to talk clearly about our actions than about our receptivity because language is a tool we devise for acting on the environment (which, of course, includes other persons). By language we define, record, specify, and classify all kinds of objects and reduce the world to an order that we can work in and upon effectively. Any of us can think of apt examples of these two modes of being, but Deikman's are as good as any. The stereotypical male cab driver in rush hour is a fine instance of the action mode. Note how he is constantly making accurate discriminations in which he recognizes the shapes and boundaries of things around him (other vehicles, pedestrians, traffic police, etc.) and braking a split second before disaster. See how sharply he focuses on his goal. He is thinking more or less logically (except, perhaps, when he discusses politics with his passenger) and is acting and reacting with what we all hope will continue to be clear and lucid discrimination. On the other hand, Deikman suggests, a monk who is engaged in meditation is quite different. He is receptive. He is trying to become selfless (to lose awareness of the shape and boundary of himself). It is true that to reach this point he may have begun by concentrating quite clearly and "mindfully" upon some object, but this was not the final purpose of his discrimination; rather he has sought to achieve that stillness of thought in which differences vanish.

The monk finally abandons logic and language, happily merges in the infinite, is relaxed, and enjoys an experience of pure receptivity about which he can afterward say almost nothing.

Let us note in passing that the receptive mode is not necessarily a rejection of the world of particular things (although it can be used for this), but is a different way of being *in* the world.

All of us are equipped to be both active and receptive, and ordinarily we alternate these modes of being: we are receptive in order to become active or as a relaxation from activity.

Deikman has adapted some meditative techniques in order to experiment with them, and he has studied much of the literature about physiological examinations of Zen masters, yogins, and adepts of Transcendental Meditation. The result is his conviction that meditation may be understood as a way of developing the receptive mode of being.

He reports that many of his experimental subjects have said that their meditative efforts enabled them to "see" colors more brightly and although, in some sense, they felt that objects had become more real, their sensitivity to boundaries had grown weaker—they were less aware of being quite separate from the objects they were using to focus attention. Further, his subjects felt that they had learned something in their moments of receptivity that seemed valuable, but they could never say what it was. Incidentally, Deikman has noted that artificial stimulation by the use of LSD or other substances of the sort often produces the same effects: a decrease in self-other discrimination, non-logical thought, and vivid awareness of colors, but diminished precision in the perception of boundaries, a loss of interest in "reality-testing," and parasympathetic dominance.

Here, then, we have an analysis of the working of meditation as a change from one mode of relating to things (the active) to another (the receptive). A question that must be faced is whether there is not, for each of these modes, a spectrum of degrees or stages running from healthy to unhealthy. For instance, can normal activity become hyperactivity? If so, the remedy may be the deliberate cultivation of the receptive mode. Can receptivity shift into a form of passivity that is no longer genuinely receptive but is rather a discounting of the reality of the world? If so, it may be useful to earn some blisters as we dig potatoes.

It may be worth asking whether the manner in which we use our modes of being depends on how we value the world and our existence in it—in short, on our assumptions or wishes about the meaning and value of human life. Persons whose fear of the world and of their own finitude in it leads them to recoil from it may be inclined to escape into the receptive and inactive mode in order at last to withdraw from the world, while those whose fear or obsession drives them toward domination may reject pure receptivity and escape into frenzied activity.

Perhaps nature has shown a kind of wisdom in endowing us with the power for both modes, and an emphasis on either one is a form of aberration. If so, neither is superior and both are necessary for the well-functioning person.

The so-called "split brain" hypothesis echoes some of what we have just been saying, although at present it must be admitted that the speculation surrounding it is very often debatable. In essence this is the view that certain skills and functions are localized in particular segments of the brain and that the brain has two hemispheres or halves, each of which does a distinct job.

In the early nineteen-sixties, researchers working with more than four hundred patients who had suffered brain damage discovered that certain kinds of mental processes that dealt with awareness of space seemed to be affected by injury to the right side of the brain.[16] Later studies have developed this thesis further, and Joseph Bogen summarizes an opinion that the left half of the brain, in most persons, seems to control functions that may be called "propositional"—logic, rational speech, and what may be termed linear or consecutive thinking—while the other half governs such functions as enjoyment of music and poetry, and the perception of images and patterns.

Lest we push this difference of function too far, it is worth noting that there is some evidence that both halves of the brain are at first capable of performing any of these activities, and that if one half is damaged the other may assume at least some of its work. Nevertheless, some researchers are convinced that there is a fairly clear division of labor between the halves of the brain, one side being the rationalist in us and the other the intuitive aestheticist.

Bogen attributes many of our experiences of inner tension to this "split" in function, including the all too familiar struggle of "head" against "heart." Above all, he finds here a possible source of two very important but different kinds of thinking: the analytic, discursive, and logical, and, on the other hand, the synthetic, non-verbal, alogical.

If this hypothesis is supported by further research, it may well be that the main effect of certain drugs and of some meditational practices is the subduing of the usually dominant hemisphere, associated with logic and verbalization, and the allowing of the other to become temporarily supreme. The difference is not one of truth versus error, of "higher" or "lower" consciousness, but simply between two sorts of thinking that are complementary but usually out of balance.

Nor would it be hard to see why an imbalance occurs favoring the rational half of the brain. The working of this side enables us to recognize and survive the dangers of the world, to wrest a living from it, to plan, predict, and avoid. But the value of the other half is recognized without argument by anyone who delights in turning from the business of the day to sink appreciatively in the sweet tyranny of Beethoven's Sixth Symphony.

Both the "bimodal consciousness" and "split brain" theories, then, suggest that the normal operations of our brain include two principal forms: a logical kind of thought and perception, criticism, analysis, and rational interpretation; and an alogical, synthetic kind of apprehension that sees things uncritically as wholes or patterns which it does not dissect. For convenience, and without intending a value judgment, we may call the first "linear" thinking and the other "holistic."

A charming example of the difference between these two kinds of thought is provided by Dorothy Lee's study of the language pattern of the Trobriand Islanders and that of their neighbors, the Dobuans. She has overheard them discussing sex together, and reports what she heard.

The Dobuans, it seems, are very much like most of us: they see things "linearly" most of the time, and this means that they take it for granted that the act of sexual intercourse is a cause of procreation. The Trobrianders, on the other hand, seem to have developed a language and style of communication that is based on a "holistic" way of seeing things. They do not think in terms of cause and effect, but in terms of wholes, of entire patterns.

Where Dobuans and we might say that a certain person was a "good gardener" and use a noun and an adjective to speak about this, the Trobrianders do not linguistically separate "good" and "gardener" but use a word that means both. "Good" is not a detachable quality, but part of the whole reality. If the gardener ceases to be good, they have a new word for the person because he or she is now a new entity; he or she is not the old gardener without the quality of goodness, but a sort of fresh creation: "bad gardener." Thus everything the Trobriander speaks about (or thinks about) is a self-contained entity that does not change into something else but is replaced by something else. As Dorothy Lee remarks, a ripe yam does not "become" overripe; rather, the overripe yam is another thing and has another name.

The Trobriand way of seeing and speaking has a consequence in practical life. Where the rest of us may select a goal and then ask what actions will accomplish it, the Trobriander conceives of a total pattern of events that includes the goal, and having elected to bring the pattern about, he or she performs the acts that are parts of it.

This is why the Trobriand discussion of sex amuses the Dobuans. As Lee says, "Though intercourse is a necessary preliminary to conception, it is not [for the Trobrianders] the cause of conception."[17] That is to say, the intercourse and the conception are simply elements in a total pattern, and the Trobriander thinks of the whole, not of the events in sequence.

As one can imagine, discussing sex with Dobuans is a problem for the Trobriand people, and the latter find themselves being teased about their "peculiar" view. When this happens, according to Lee, the Trobrianders appear embarrassed, "giving the impression that they [are] trying to maintain unquestioningly a stand in which they had to believe."[18]

It is clearly possible to organize our interpretation of the world around either the holistic or the linear kind of thinking, and it is also possible to argue that neither alone is adequate for all purposes. What is important at the moment is the suggestion that the holistic function of the brain is the source of those meditative insights that seem so remarkable when they first occur. To see in this way—immediately, intuitively, and without parts or sequences—may be an adventure that seems to lift any of us to a higher realm of knowledge.

Many meditators will agree with the tentative conclusion we seem to be led to here: there are values in those altered states that they can achieve through their discipline, but there is really no higher truth to be gained—only a fresh perspective. Others, however, advance some important claims for new "truths" they have found; for examining truth-claims, one must turn to the tool of philosophy

Some Additional Recent Speculations About Subjective Experience

Roberto Assagioli

A particularly inventive therapist, Roberto Assagioli, has recently captured attention with some ideas similar to suggestions in my last chapter and a practice of psychotherapy based on them. Assagioli recognizes that our ways of knowing things may broadly be termed "analytical" and "intuitive." When we are thinking analytically we actually know things piece by piece; we see each part of our object (whether that is a system of philosophy, a shopping list, or a lawnmower), and we see and understand the relation of one part to another so that whatever we have in mind is a connected set of parts. Thus we may learn a new procedure in mathematics step by step until at last we are familiar with each step and with the way the steps complement each other to achieve a result.

Intuition, by contrast, is synthetic: that is, it puts everything together in one flash. It sees both things and processes as wholes.

These two ways of understanding (which we might call the Dobuan and Trobriand styles, respectively) may also be associated with what we have said about "left" and "right" halves of the brain or "bimodal" functioning.

Assagioli believes that both these ways of mental working are important and that neither is more natural or more mysterious than the other. Nor is one of them entirely reliable while the other alone is prone to error. The intuitive may seem to us more compelling by its very immediacy, but not only is it as liable to mistakes as its alternative, it actually needs to be checked by analytical reason because it is not self-critical at all.

Because a complementary use of both kinds of knowing is valuable for a complete understanding, Assagioli has developed a technique that he calls "psychosynthesis," by which he tries to enrich us by making the two kinds of thinking mutually helpful. He finds that, for most people, he must first teach how to arouse the synthetic or intuitive.

To do this, he says, we must temporarily suspend our more common analytical way of viewing things, first expunging from consciousness such experiences as sensation, emotion, and discursive thought. Once this is done we have only to await quietly the spontaneous coming of intuitive sensitivity "which in successful cases becomes a contact with and even an identification of the subject with the looked-for experience of reality or truth."[19]

We see here a secularized version of popular meditative method. There is, however, no thought here of reaching a supranormal state of mind, but simply of making better use of all the mind's capacities. This is a therapeutic, not a religious, frame of reference. The complete and healthy individual, according to this theory, learns to "know" in both the analytical and intuitive (or holistic) fashion, and only when both ways are working well may he or she be said to know fully.

Michael Polanyi

Another interesting writer on a subject close to ours is the philosopher of science, Michael Polanyi. He argues that the human mind works with two levels or dimensions of understanding, one of which he calls "tacit" and the other "explicit."[20]

Explicit understanding is akin to what we have called linear or logical reasoning. It is a rearranging of what we know until we see the "sense" of it, but this "sense" is achieved by our grasping the relation of parts to each other. Thus it is like Assagioli's "analytic" function. When the "sense" or pattern of our object becomes clear to us we are likely (even without Assagioli's therapeutic discipline) suddenly to feel that we "see" the whole. We may speak of the truth "dawning" on us. This is because the *Gestalt* or whole that we have finally apprehended becomes spontaneously clear and is seen as somehow more than just the sum of the parts. Its very wholeness is a new datum, a new fact not numbered among the parts. To see this wholeness is to see with immediacy a complete entity and not just a set of ingredients. Thus we may construct a cake by putting together carefully the various items called for in the recipe, and we could continue to think of the final product as that set of ingredients. What we actually do, however, is finally see the cake as a new and whole thing.

Now, this total grasp of pattern or meaning or wholeness rests upon the function Polanyi calls "tacit" understanding. This is, in some ways, a deeper, broader readiness to understand, and it underlies our "explicit" or logical, piece-by-piece grasp of things. Even when putting the ingredients of the cake together, we understand their relationship because we already *tacitly* have the concept of the cake.

When a friend speaks to us, we *explicitly* understand each word, but we would not understand the entire sentence or fathom its meaning if we still had only a set of separate words. It is because we *tacitly* possess the full meaning that the words can bring that meaning to our mind. Communication evokes or brings to the surface an understanding we already tacitly possessed—and if we do not possess it, no combination of words will produce it. Or, rather, the work of constructing a tacit understanding that is new to us will be difficult and we may have to hear or read the words many times before tacit understanding is formed. When it is, it will lie ready for reawakening when a suitable set of words is presented to us again. (Those familiar with Zen discussions of the use of language and its power to evoke the "unborn" or the "original face" in us will see a parallel concept here, as will those who know the thought of Saint Augustine on the subject of Christian education.)

Another dimension of Polanyi's discussion of our modes of understanding is his distinction between "focal" and "subsidiary" attention, and this brings us close to some earlier observations about meditative methods. When we use our ordinary rationality we attend to the parts of whatever we are trying to understand. Thus translators may work with one word at a time as they try to render a difficult sentence into their own language, or mechanics may examine each part of a motor as they try to determine how it fits together. Here our "focus" is on the separate parts and their relationship, and so long as it is such, the real meaning or purpose of the thing under study will partly escape our grasp. We will have a string of individually comprehended words or a fully assembled motor, but we will not yet understand the sentence or know the use of the motor.

For full understanding we must eventually command the whole, the total pattern of things. To do this we must focus not on the parts but on the complete entity, seeing the parts only in a subsidiary or peripheral way. We must direct our "focal" attention on the whole, our "subsidiary" on the elements of it.

Here again, then, we see an attempt to describe our mental life in terms of duality of function, but one that achieves the highest results when synthesized. Obviously, many forms of meditation aim at so fixing and narrowing our attention that what Polanyi calls "subsidiary" awareness grows weaker and weaker. When this is pressed far enough, our attention is purely "focal" and, as we have seen, the natural process of our brain then causes the object momentarily to slip from consciousness, giving us the experience of a kind of empty focus or a seemingly infinite, contentless consciousness.

For meditation theory, our grasp of a new *Gestalt*—the whole meaning of life—follows the experience of this empty focus, and as we enjoy that sense of seeing "All" we may also be aware of a subsidiary alertness to the individual aspects or parts. Polanyi seems to suggest that it is not the experience of focal intensity and subsidiary awareness of parts itself that is new in meditation (for this experience occurs often enough) but rather it is the nature of the focused *object* and the range of subsidiary elements that overwhelm us, for it is life, reality, the cosmos itself that is now the focus.

Like Assagioli, Polanyi would warn us, however, that we are not entitled to be dogmatically certain about either our focused understanding or our perception of the subsidiary parts, for we are still a fallible human organism whose "highest" perceptions need careful checking.

A Final Possibility

This chapter presents a selection of ideas about consciousness. Much of what has been said may be superseded by continuing study. One more approach that comes close to our subject deserves mention, although it must be admitted that many questions can be raised about it and it is an enterprise still in its infancy.

At several centers in the United States the medical procedure called hemodialysis (in effect, the purifying of the blood by removing it from the body and passing it through a machine) is being used experimentally in the treatment of chronic process schizophrenia, and some rather remarkable results have already been claimed for it.

Schizophrenia is a tormenting disease not only for those who endure it, but for those who love them. For many years physicians have wondered whether it is caused by a genetic fault or whether it arises because of something in the environment of the victim. Some researchers at the present time favor a genetic explanation, but in any case it seems *possible* that its actual occurrence rests upon a chemical malfunctioning of the body. If this is so, it would be useful to discover what goes wrong and what chemical or chemicals are responsible.

It is well known that certain drugs (such as LSD, mescaline, and amphetamines) can sometimes cause reactions very similar to schizophrenia, and it has been noted that some of the visionary experiences of quite legitimate mystics bear striking resemblance to certain schizophrenic experiences. Could it be, then, that biochemistry may offer a clue to the nature not only of schizophrenia but also of other altered states of consciousness, whether these were induced by drugs or meditation?

Almost by accident an interesting therapy for schizophrenia may have been discovered a few years ago. A patient with strong schizophrenic symptoms was treated by dialysis. She had been hallucinating and was psychotic, almost unable to relate to others, and certainly quite unable to perform her work. She had, in fact, been hospitalized serveral times within a fairly short period and was virtually immobilized. After the program of dialysis she was able to return to work and suffered no more hallucinations or delusions. Her ability to relate to others had vastly improved.

Apparently similar experiments have sometimes (not always) met with similar results. Could it be, then, that dialysis removes from the blood of some schizophrenics a chemical that is responsible for the deranged perception and conception of the victim? Perhaps some persons manufacture too much of some natural body chemical, and perhaps there are ways—meditation among them—of stimulating this imbalance temporarily.

We are in a realm of sheer speculation here, but it opens a line of investigation that probably is worth pursuing.

Conclusion

We have briefly examined a set of theories that would try to account for altered states of consciousness and interpret their role in the functioning of the human being. Regression to an infantile (or even embryonic) state of mind, cosmicizing the ego, redirection of *libido*, the manipulation of our physical chemistry, a "blinking" of consciousness caused by overconcentration and followed by detachment from assumptions that had formed our identity—all these "explanations" have their own degrees of plausibility.

Possibly richer in suggestion were other ideas: dehabituation leading to a freshness of vision and experience and a sense of liberation; the reversal of the usual order of dominance in our "bimodal consciousness" so that the receptive is asserted in place of the active, and the "left" brain with its holistic, alogical, intuitive mode of thought is allowed to rule in place of the "right" brain with its analytical, logical approach.

The final weeding out of error in these theories, and a satisfying synthesis of what remains, are not yet possible, although some lines of convergence seem clear. Enough has certainly been said to make it clear that in altered consciousness we are dealing with something worth studying and deserving to be stripped of the mystique that tends to make questions taboo.

5

Philosophical Critique

Many philosophers would argue that, having described the physiology and psychology of meditation with its states of consciousness, we need go no further. Indeed, they would contend that it is meaningless to speak of these experiences as if they were more than psycho-physical events. So cheap a dismissal, however, will hardly persuade the enthusiast who sees profound "truth" as somehow disclosed in what has happened within him, and it should not satisfy the sympathetic inquirer. After all, the experience of seeing a cloud and indulging in fantasies about its shape is also a physio-psychological process, yet it is not meaningless to ask whether one person sees the cloud more clearly than another or whether the experience of delight is not a significant human achievement.

Ontological Claims

Norman Melchert has examined some of the most impressive claims made by mystics and meditators concerning the relation between their most intense experiences and "Being" or reality itself.[1] He distinguishes the experience he wants to discuss as characterized by "disappearance of the ego," "union with the One," or "union with God"—experiences generally called "enlightenment," "satori," or "unitary consciousness." This is obviously one of the most remarkable of all "altered states," and the claim that it really *is* the kind of union described, the kind of abolition of "self," is perhaps the most remarkable claim made for any kind of awareness.

According to those who report this experience, it is "nonconceptual." That is to say, it is not an idea or an "understanding" which comes to us in words. It contains no sensory content and it cannot be expressed verbally. Furthermore, it is non-connative, or marked by detachment from all possible objects of desire. A person enjoying such an experience feels free from any anxiety or restraint, and no sense of "I" or "mine" remains to him or her. We have already examined some ways of describing this kind of experience and have seen that psychology and psycho-biology are inclined to see it as something to be interpreted with no reference to any supernatural categories. Melchert agrees, and opines that the unitive, egoless, transcendent experience of meditative consciousness is as natural as apple pie.

Persons who experience this unusual state are often, however, inclined to think they have wrought something more wonderful than apple pie, and Melchert quotes several of them to support the view that the experience often leads its subjects to conclude that they have crossed a boundary that effectively excludes the rest of us. "The end result is a knowledge on the part of the experiencer that his being and nature are incomparably greater than they had previously seemed to be."[2]

The first step in a critique of Melchert's claim is a reminder that some students of Western philosophy will find interesting. One of the most influential and perceptive of European philosophers, Immanuel Kant, argued convincingly that we cannot reach conclusions about the "I," or about the self that thinks, by analyzing its actual thinking or mental experience.[3] Melchert says that this is relevant to the mystical experience—one cannot know very much that is conclusive about the mystic simply by examining his experience; and neither can the mystic himself. The experience and the person having it are, of course, intimately related but are not so identical that conclusions about the one are infallible guides to conclusions about the other.

To illustrate this point we may note that in the unitary experience (when we feel that "all is One") there is no sense of our own separate selfhood and we seem to ourselves to be limitless. On the basis of this feeling, we are sometimes (if we are mystically inclined) led to suppose that we are *really* quite without limits; that is, we are infinite, we are God. However, this is to make a mistake like the one Kant diagnosed; it is to suppose, without good grounds, that we can reach a valid inference about ourselves on the basis of a subjective experience; it is to equate what seems to be the character of a state of mind with what *is* the character of the person having the state of mind, and this is simply not something that can validly be done. To put this as plainly as possible, *we may know that we can cultivate an experience that recognizes no limits and no selfhood or otherness; we cannot infer from this experience that there are no limits, selfhood, and otherness.*

Why, then, is it so common for the person who experiences unitary consciousness to make the false leap to a conclusion that "all *really* is One"? No doubt the answer is partly that the liberation experienced when one has become "Absolute" is exhilarating, especially for persons who were discontented with their former state of being, despising the "self" they thought themselves to be, or afraid of the dangers inherent in a world where there are other persons and things they cannot control. The shortest way to overcome fear of a savage dog is to believe oneself to *be* the dog, or to produce a state of mind in which the dog and the self have become one.

Some persons have an acute need to escape the sense of individual selfhood. The prominent and well-published psychotherapist, R. D. Laing, has said that people who lack a strong sense of identity are often inclined to fear that they will somehow be "swallowed" or absorbed and robbed of reality in relationships with more powerful persons, that their tenuous hold upon existence and independence will be broken by the sheer force of other personalities. Such a man or woman knows only too well what it means to be limited and finite, to feel daily the terrifying danger of being depersonalized. As a defense against these catastrophes the person's weak ego may resort to schizoid or even schizophrenic behavior, including the attempt to obliterate the realities of others, or at least to diminish the threatening personality in them by reducing them to the status of mere "things." In extreme cases the person may finally manage to view all objective reality, even his or her own self as an objective fact, as something like an illusion, detaching the self from it altogether.[4]

It is possible, then, that for some the great attraction of very intense forms of meditative consciousness is partly that such meditation can produce an effect strikingly similar to the schizoid. One escapes possible engulfment by becoming the Cosmic Engulfer, enlarging one's reality to the size of the universe or, which amounts to much the same, losing one's particular personal reality altogether. In this way one may eliminate threats from "outside" by erasing the distinction between outside and inside. Of course, to achieve this effect one must believe that the experience of no-self and no-limit is more than just a state of the psyche.

It may be worth noting that the scriptures of Buddhism represent the Buddha, before his enlightenment, as a young prince whose disenchantment with palatial life occurs after he has awakened to the inevitability of death, disease, and old age. He wonders why people can carry on with life as if nothing were wrong. We are, he thinks, like children laughing in a burning house. This appears to be a fine description of what some have called "ontological anxiety," the state of mind in which the dangers to life so dominate us that we turn to one of the escape mechanisms described above.

It may be, then, that many who interpret their altered states of consciousness as having ontological value are the victims of oppressive anxiety. In any event, Melchert has argued that they seem to be the perpetrators of a logical error.

The fallacious inference that "all is One" because "I have experienced oneness" is probably made easier by a confusion about knowing. "It is a truism," says Melchert, "that 'if you know, you can't be wrong.'"[5] The mystics seem to themselves to *know* something now that was hidden before, and to know it with a directness and certainty that transcends any other knowing they have ever enjoyed. But the question is, what *is* a state of "knowing"? Is there any condition in which what we know is unmistakably confirmed by the mere fact or manner of our knowing it? Is there any self-authenticating form of knowledge?

It has sometimes been argued that a condition of knowing is beyond criticism if it is outside the range of concepts, words, and ideas. If we "know" intuitively, without any rational process involved, we must know directly, without mediation of thoughts and words, and therefore unquestionably. If our knowing is of a "whole" and contains no dividedness, no alternatives, then it is impossible for a question to arise, and if no question arises, our knowledge must be complete and accurate.

This belief in an unquestionable sort of knowing is, alas, patently absurd. It is quite true that we may reach a state of mind in which our mind itself cannot question its content, but there is no necessary connection between this state and the guarantee that our mind is correct. Unquestioning conviction has led to many a catastrophe, and the experience of being right beyond question, single-mindedly and joyously filled with clear awareness, has sometimes been a mark of insanity. As Melchert remarks, "The basic truth . . . is that there is no such thing as a 'state of knowing,' if by this is meant an experiential state the characteristics of which are sufficient to guarantee that it really constitutes knowledge."[6]

To put this plainly, *any* mental state is only a mental state, and the belief that it entails a knowledge that is beyond error is, and must always be, an act of faith however many people affirm it.

A fallacy similar to that which Melchert points to in the mystics' conviction about their "knowing" occurs sometimes in aesthetics. Some persons seek a painting's "meaning" or "significance" outside the work itself, in the intention of the artist. This may be called the "intentional fallacy," for (even supposing we may know the artist's real intention) it is not an appraisal of the art, but of the artist. Others seek the meaning of the work neither in the work itself nor in the artist's intention, but in the spontaneous response that the art generates in themselves. This has been called the "affective fallacy" because, once again, it is not the work that is really being assessed, but the response of the viewer. The critics who commit the affective fallacy are locked up within themselves, reducing all objectivity to their own subjectivity and therefore ultimately losing the integrity and reality of the work of art. Similarly, the mystic or meditator who identifies the truth about reality with his or her own mental state is committing the affective fallacy, or something very like it.

We are not denying that people may engender in themselves a state of awareness which presents itself as universal, unitary, godlike; a state beyond all distinctions of subject and object, of knowing or not knowing, of perceiving or not perceiving. Our contention is simply that such a state, whatever its psychological benefits to the distraught, does not dissolve the world around us, does not bring us any certain knowledge of what or who we are, and may, indeed, even bring us misunderstanding.

This first criticism of truth-claims will offend many because it reduces the remarkable experience of mystics to the level of the purely natural and robs it of any transcendent significance. John Blofeld has written, "When we sit in meditation and upon occasion attain great bliss—is there nothing supernatural in that?"[7] And with a little surprise at what seems to be an excessive naïveté, the philosopher must answer: "Nothing at all! It is as natural as apple pie."

Superiority of Intuition over Reason

Another claim often made for altered states of consciousness is that in being intuitive they are something more than ordinarily direct, necessarily true apprehensions of reality. Intuition, it is said, is *immediate* "knowing," while reason gives us only indirect "knowing *about*" something. It follows that whatever is apprehended intuitively does not only represent but *is* the truth, and thus it is utterly beyond the criticism of mere reason, which lives in a more distant and humbler level.

This point of view has, of course, been attacked often enough by devotees of reason, whose common riposte has been that intuition certainly lies outside reason, but below it, and tends to be the refuge of those afraid to live with the undogmatic uncertainties which reason inevitably produces. A lucid and fairly representative statement on behalf of rationality has been offered by Michael Oakeshott, perhaps the most perceptive of modern English political philosophers and observers of the general human scene.[8]

Oakeshott characterizes the chief intuitionist critique of rational thought thus: "Thinking, it is said, is the qualification of existence by an idea. Without an idea there can be no thinking."[9] This means that a constructed thing, a product of the mind—an idea—intrudes ungraciously between the thinker and the world so that he or she knows the world only at second hand. Indeed, the thinker does not know the world at all, for all that he or she knows is the idea. In this the thinker is surpassed by the intuitionist who gets the idea out of the way and knows reality without any such misleading prism. Oakeshott hints that such a distinction, beside being invidious, is itself quite as arbitrary as the thinker's idea is said to be. It is to make an idea a subjective event of a different sort than the intuition without showing that it is so, without showing that the event called intuition is not itself as liable to mislead. An idea is a tool by which we loosely relate to reality, while intuition is supposed to be reality itself—but Oakeshott finds this unconvincing.

There is much to be said for Oakeshott's judgment, but it is easy to understand the attraction of intuition. If one surfs, the immediate experience of encounter with the sea can be an exhilarating thing. One is simply *there*, moved by the motion of the water and quite at one with it. But the surfer or swimmer actually knows less about the ocean than someone who has used reason to study it. The surfer may, indeed, be endangered by his or her very sense of unity with it. Further, the surfer's apparently direct knowledge of the water is not really less mediated than that of the oceanographer—it is mediated by every sense that spontaneously responds to its environment. The sea known by the oceanographer is no less the sea for its being thought about, and that person is more likely to be able to live in it safely because he or she does not mindlessly identify with it and disregard its dangers.

More precisely, Oakeshott argues that the distinction between thought and intuition appears persuasive only if one (thoughtlessly) makes thinking more limited than it is. If the term is used properly, it names a much wider range of mental processes that actually include what we have called intuition, the latter being simply one form of thought, no more mysterious or enlightened than others. In fact, intuition depends on rational thought to defend and explain itself, and "a form of experience which is unable to establish its own validity is clearly less complete than that to which it must appeal for this purpose."[10]

Michael Oakeshott wrote his criticism before very much was known about the "split" character of the human brain, but much of what he says may well be supported by our increasing knowledge of this organ. The debate between intuitionists and rationalists appears to be between two halves of the brain, and it begins to appear as though we need to consider either side alone as insufficient. Indeed it may be argued that neither intuition nor reason is a "higher" form of consciousness than the other, for they are complementary. Synthesis is required for a fully human mental life, and it is notable that in great artists, poets, and scientists (and even philosophers, occasionally) we often find clear instances of thought that embrace both intuition and critical reason without the spurious denigration of either.

The philosopher must point out, further, that even when an efficient synthesis has been achieved, even when we have extended our total brain to the limit of its capacity, we shall still be operating, rationally and intuitively, only within the limits of that brain. A simple act of surgery can curtail either aspect of our mental life. The really intriguing question emerges only when this is recognized: is there a center of value, of creative intention and action beyond all our brains? Are we, to put it shortly, the evolutionary creatures of a deity? No certain answer appears possible to this question, but it can be explored only with the aid of both intuition and reason.

Perhaps we should acknowledge that the rabid intuitionist has generally replied to criticism that the critic has not had the proper experience: "You haven't had my state of consciousness, so you don't know what you're talking about." This is by no means certainly true, but even when it is, the rationalist has replied, "I haven't had *dementia praecox*, either, but I know it's not good!" If the debate is conducted at all, the person of reason seems to have an advantage: the opponent supports the validity of rational argument by resorting to it.

The Primacy of Subjecthood over Agenthood

There is one assumption that is shared by those who are convinced of the truth-value of their mystical or meditative experience and by a vast company of philosophers: it is that the human being is principally a *subject* (a thinker or experiencer), and as a subject he or she comes to know whatever reality there is. It can be argued, however, that this belief about us, obvious and axiomatic as it must seem to many, is the root of an enormous amount of error.

How can one possibly *not* consider himself or herself principally a subject? What alternative is there? The French philosopher René Descartes, who did much to shape the European philosophical tradition that followed him, tried to sift his knowledge to find some one thing that was utterly beyond the reach of doubt, and what he found was "I think: therefore I am." His existence *as a subject*, as a thinker or as consciousness, was the only "unquestionable" ground on which he could build a system of understanding. Surely whatever else may be in doubt, we *know* that we are awareness, that we think and experience, that before all else and more certain than all else we are subjects.

But consider where this leads us. If the one fundamental truth about me is that I am a subject, the questions soon arise, "Are there, then, any *objects*? Are there any subjects other than myself?" "How can I be sure that my apparent seeing, hearing, knowing of things and persons is *more* than an event of my subjectivity, more than an illusion fabricated by my mind?" What a subject knows is an *idea*, an impression, an intuition: is there anything outside these things? I look at you and am filled with the impression of your form. But are you really there, or are you just a product of my creative imagination?

In other words, when we begin with the assumption that subjectivity (or experience) is primary, we always eventually stumble into the age-old problem of the relation of subject and object, of myself and all others.

The healthy, stouthearted person has no problem here. He or she scornfully rejects our question and growls, "I always knew philosophy was a disease." This person *knows* that friends really exist, that the world is full of things that are quite certainly there whether his or her consciousness is aware of them or not. Oh, things may not be as impenetrably solid as we once thought, but however they are constructed, of what intricate patterns of relationship between matter and energy and so on, they are *there*. Unfortunately, some of us cannot or will not settle for this blunt and cheerful faith.

Indeed, many persons find a certain relief in the notion that their subjectivity is all the reality there is. This means that the dangers of a pluralistic world have vanished, and whatever tragedies there may be, whatever violence and hostility, are but shadow plays within the Mind that creates such fancies. If subjectivity is the one indisputable reality, there need be no object at all. All that exists may be ideas, feelings, intuitions.

Beginning with the assumption that, whatever else may be true, I am primarily a subject, the philosopher may erect a wondrous world-view in which everything is some form of "idea," and the mystic may joyfully conclude that his or her experience of absolute oneness, pure consciousness free of all content, is the "ultimate truth" of reality. Such a pleasant, internally coherent system of belief can be established in this way, reinforced (apparently) by intuitive experience, that it is hardly surprising that a great many people have taken refuge there from the slings and arrows of outrageous fortune.

Subjectivism (or Idealism) certainly offers some advantages. It is easier to be gentle and benign toward persons when you have deprived them of the uncomfortable angularity of their real independence, their irreducible otherness. The conflict of personalities is mitigated when you no longer believe in the final reality of persons. A sweet compassion can be cultivated when it does not have to reckon with the real ugliness, the stolidly actual viciousness of very genuine beings. Even the irritation evoked by one's importunate spouse and offspring may be softened when one's family is merely a complex idea in the Cosmic Mind! But it is just here that one of the theological objections to subjectivism arises (for which we shall consider Martin Buber's thought in chapter seven), and it is despite these benefits that John Macmurray, a respected but too often neglected British philosopher, challenges the root assumption on which they rest.[11]

Macmurray reminds us that we do not begin life as self-aware centers of consciousness who look around to see whether or not something else exists. The baby presumably becomes aware of itself as a self only after and because it has actually met things that have proven to be *other* than it; its hand meets the resistance of a crib or the tooth of the family dog, its hunger meets the aggravating otherness of a mother who is late with lunch. We begin to make distinctions in our world not by inventing them but by discovering them. We are forced to recognize that the world contains things that resist us, frustrate us, or delight us, and because of them we begin the process of discovering ourselves and then constructing a richer self.

The significance of all this is that our subjectivity is not primary but responsive; it comes to life and takes its shape not as a creator of its world but through relationship with it. We begin our experience in a situation in which neither the subject nor the object is basic, but the encounter of the two.

Because of his observation of this, Macmurray wants to begin to philosophize in a new way. Whereas much human thought begins with the assumption that the primary fact, the only undeniable reality, is our subjectivity, Macmurray offers us the view that this makes no sense whatever of our actual experience of life. By contrast, what is real is relationship, and upon this rock we must build our self-understanding.

Once our consciousness has come to birth we may, of course, do many things with it and alter it in various ways, but we should not deceive ourselves that an altered state of consciousness is anything more than the end of a program of self-manipulation. Fully healthy consciousness that is still in touch with reality will always be sensitive to that reality around it. Contentless consciousness is quite producible and has its uses, but it may be like an electrical short-circuit if it becomes too attractive or important to us.

From this observation of the dependent nature of our subjectivity, John Macmurray takes a further step. To relate is to be active, at least in a modest way, and if relating is primary then the human being is primarily an agent or actor and only secondarily and derivatively a subject. In other words, our subjecthood arises as a result of our agenthood, our acting upon and meeting with the world about us, and it functions (when it does so well) as a means of evaluating, planning, understanding, and improving subsequent action. *Subjecthood is dependent upon and exists for the sake of agenthood.* This is why authentic love, while it must seek knowledge, is more fundamental to human reality than mere knowledge. And this is why, if we divorce our subjectivity from the world of objects and other subjects, it will construct an inevitably false world view.

The "bimodal consciousness" theory, as we have seen, contends that the two modes available to us are the active and the receptive. The former tends to become dominant because its operation is essential for our survival—we simply must wrest a living from the earth. This appears to be in line with Macmurray's opinion that the active mode (agenthood) is primary in the well-functioning person, and the receptive mode (subjecthood) exists as a response to it and for the sake of its refinement.

It is only as agents that we can become truly personal, since personhood is a product not of isolation but of relation to other persons. Robinson Crusoe on his island, and a hermit in a Himalayan cave, are persons only because they have had personal relations and have lived their agenthood.

Our subjectivity exists, then, "within" and for the sake of our agenthood, and the proper pattern of our living will be an alternation of doing and thinking, including within thinking all our subjective performance, even, in Oakeshott's fashion, our intuiting. This means that our lives will follow a pattern of "withdrawal and return" to and from action and relationship, but the withdrawal must be for the sake of the return or we shall unbalance our living.

Since awareness is so intrinsically embedded in a world outside ourselves, how does it happen that we are seduced into subjectivism? Among other possibilities, Macmurray offers a suggestion that it may be due to our propensity for arranging our sense experience in an order of priority, giving first place to vision. Most of us spend little thought on what it would be like to be deprived of taste, and many of us assume (mistakenly, according to some theorists) that to lose our vision is more grievous than to lose our hearing. So vision is the sense we prize most highly, and it becomes the model on which we build our language and our philosophy.

Vision, however, is an experience that separates us from the object. If you place something against your eye you can no longer see it. Distance is a precondition of seeing, and this means that there is room at once for doubt whether the thing seen is really there. When our thinking about ourselves and our world is based on the experience of seeing, we are already halfway into idealism (or what I have preferred, for our discussion, to call subjectivism), because vision brings us nothing of the object except an image. To make matters worse, our imagination can create images as readily as our eyes can capture them, and this increases our doubt about the objective reality of what we see.

From infancy we are conditioned to emphasize seeing. Who of us has not had cautious parents warn us (especially when they *incautiously* set us loose in a toy store), "*Look*, don't touch!"? In many cultures this emphasis reaches such a point that in greeting one another persons avoid physical contact and exchange either a bow or some other signal of greeting.

What makes all this a little odd is that vision is by no means our most indispensable sense. Although some studies seem to show that loss of hearing can be more serious than blindness, what would really destroy us would be the loss of our sense of touch. If we felt nothing, if we never knew the resistance of the ground beneath our feet or the chair on which we sat, it might well be impossible to continue living. Touch is the most important of all our senses, but touch is precisely that sense which involves active relationship. To touch anything is to act upon it, to be forced to acknowledge its resistant otherness; and a philosophy that began with this fact would therefore end not in subjectivism but in relationalism—in the acknowledgment that life is being-in-touch-with-others.

What John Macmurray invites us to do, then, is to recognize that subjectivism cannot explain why the illusion (or whatever it is) arises that we are a single, limited individual surrounded by a world of objects and other subjects as real as ourselves, and to realize that this plurality is more enduring than any one of us is. On the contrary, if we begin with the fact of otherness and accept touch rather than vision as our primary experience, we are launched into a philosophy of relationship that places such experiences as mystical oneness or "non-dual consciousness" in proper perspective as acceptable moments of relief from the actual complexities of life. These moments may, however, mislead us by tempting us to escape reality and disavow the basic truth into which we were born.

The criticism here of the more exotic states of consciousness is not, then, that they are necessarily useless, but that they must always be deliberately used to serve the purpose of action. If they are sought for their own sake, or if some kind of consciousness is taken to be "reality itself" and more important than action, then we have abandoned the truth which brought us into being and have embraced what we must sadly but insistently call a delusion. Separate, individual consciousness is born in experience; it is only by an editing of experience and a distortion of the balance of consciousness that we can persuade ourselves that "unitary consciousness" is of supreme importance.

The "Still Point" versus the "Eternal Process"

Many people feel uncomfortable in a world of dualities such as self and other, here and there, life and death, and so on. They must try to release the tension between these poles (or binary oppositions, as Structuralists like to call them) either by welding them into a synthesis or by emphasizing one at the expense of the other. For such persons a critical question is: is reality (the universe, God, Brahman, or whatever they call the total of existents) one or many? Is it a perfect stillness, unchanging in any way, or is it an endless motion, a process, a becoming?

The weight of philosophy, both Eastern and Western, has tended to favor stillness over process and oneness over plurality. A few attempts have been made (in Judaism and Christianity, for example) to express the vision that what is real is both One and many, and that it is a process whose "'unchangingness" is simply its fidelity to itself. But until the emergence of the so-called Process Philosophy of fairly recent times, the adoration of stillness, the identification of perfection with that which was always and in all important respects the same, has tended to triumph among philosophers and theologians, even though common sense has led most people to live as if it were not true.

Among others, Henri Bergson, Alfred North Whitehead, and Charles Hartshorne have led a movement in celebration of motion and have argued that it is more fundamental than stillness. What follows in this section is inevitably heavily dependent on their work.[12]

An adequate view of reality must take seriously all that we experience, and even leave room for the possibility that there is more than even that vast sum. Pain is a fact as surely as is pleasure, anxiety as surely as peace. I experience continuity with my past, and for this reason can sometimes account for what I am by what I decided or did when I was younger. However, I also experience discontinuity with my past: I can no longer listen with the same joy to music that seemed to me once the epitome of art, and I cannot recover the ecstasy that cotton candy once induced in me. I have changed, yet it is still I. One can define oneself simply in terms of the present moment, thus eliminating process, or one can do it in terms of a dynamic continuity, comprising a process of growth and decay. To think of oneself simply as belonging to the recent moment, however, is to make no sense of what one *is* in that moment: we are all that we have been, and even our future casts its shadow before it, because the pressures and inclinations that will shape us tomorrow are already at work in us today. I am most surely a *process*, a becoming that will be still only when I am dead. Yet that process is not chaos but has a fairly high degree of consistency within itself; it is quite true to say both that I am who I was yesterday, and that I am today a new person.

Because the most intense of meditative experiences are likely to be states of consciousness from which change and objectivity have been eliminated, many who have had them feel that they have seen the illusoriness of change and have, for a moment, known what reality is "really" like: it is a still point, it is a fullness which leaves no room for change. Change belongs to a "lower" realm of experience than Truth, and our liberation from its deception is the greatest goal of life. This means, of course, that change, motion, process (powerful elements of our ordinary experience) are less than absolutely real, and that various forms of verbal juggling may be used to discountenance them. But the very act of affirming that stillness is truth is a violation of stillness! To proclaim that "all is One" is, in the act of making the proclamation, really to affirm that all is *not* One, for there are the affirmer, the affirmation, and presumably he or she to whom the affirmation is addressed.

In short, to say that "reality" is without movement or change is simply a logical blunder, because the statement itself is a movement and brings about a change in the history of what has been said.

This means that although one can manipulate consciousness and achieve a state in which there is neither object nor self-awareness and in which there is no motion, this is an experience *abstracted from* the fullness of reality rather than a *complete* experience of it.

It may be that everything that exists is somehow "One," but if so it is not the oneness of unitary consciousness, for existence includes the divided consciousness as well; it incorporates otherness as well as identity. To put this differently, reality's oneness is shaped by the reality of manyness. If this were not so, it would make no sense for the seeker of unity to meditate at all, since this is itself a process and involves change; if oneness were the simple truth of things, there could be no possibility of an alteration even in consciousness.

That meditation may lead us to experience a pause in our awareness of flux is a fact (and, for most of us, at certain times a very beneficent fact); but that it means that only stillness is fundamentally real is obviously absurd.

Our popular conviction that whatever is perfect is changeless seems to be due largely to a prejudice which is not supported by our common experience. If the static were superior to the changing, a painted landscape, frozen forever on canvas, would be superior to the ever-changing mountain represented there; the orderliness of death would be better than the effervescence of life. But what if *life, motion,* and *growth* are the marks of perfection? What if creativity, which can only arise in the presence of some degree of tension, and constructive thought, which begins only when a problem discomforts us, are more god-like than tranquility! Those who see that process is the principal ingredient of experience, and become convinced that it is the key to understanding why we are here and why there is a world like ours, are not necessarily despisers of peace or rejecters of meditation; but they place these things in a context that profoundly relativizes their value.

Experience and Interpretation

It is sometimes claimed that certain altered forms of awareness are perfectly self-contained, uncolored by anything outside themselves, unshaped by any preliminary ideas or preconceptions: they are simply what happens when all prejudices and preconceptions are removed. They are an immediate "knowing," which owes nothing whatever to philosophy, preference, or environment. Against this contention there may be offered some experimental data seeming to indicate that the "set" (that is, the expectations, conscious or unconscious value systems, and other mental furniture) and the "setting" (the environment) in which these states arise are decisively influential at least in the way they are understood by those who have them.

One of the most lucid and attractive expositors of Tibetan Buddhism, Lama Anagarika Govinda, acknowledges the persistent undercurrent of our personal assumptions even in our mysticism. The "ultimate" mystical state is, he acknowledges, reported somewhat differently in different traditions:

> To some it is a state of isolation (*kevalatva*), of pure self-existence, to others a merging into a higher being (*sāyujyatva*) or into the impersonal state of the universal *brahman*, and again to others it is unqualified freedom and independence (*svātantrya*), etc.[13]

Govinda's own comment on this is, "It shows us that even the highest attainments may retain some individual taste—the taste of the soil from which they grew—without impairing thereby their universal value."[14]

This suggests that, in the Lama's view, it is not simply the interpretation that is shaped by our preconceptions, but the experience itself owes something to them; this raises the question whether such "ultimate" experiences are really noetic—whether they are really a knowing or understanding at all—or whether they are merely a state in which our subjectivity is unified and held in possession of something we had already begun to possess.

Some authorities are far less generous than the Lama in allowing that such experiences other than their own are of "universal value." One of the most influential books of Mahayana Buddhism is *The Awakening of Faith* attributed to Aśvaghosha, and it indicates that *samādhi*, the crowning meditative experience, may actually be misleading if it is founded on a wrong philosophy: "The samadhi of the heretics are [sic] not free from perverse views, craving, and arrogance."[15] This is a very serious charge, because it means that a lifetime of meditation may only lead us subtly astray if our beliefs are mistaken. More important for us, it would appear that the "truth" that is grasped in *samādhi* depends on the preparation of the intellect beforehand.

Many mystics have reported that they knew a moment when they broke free from all the acquired convictions, values, and fears which were their old "ego" or self-image, and found themselves free, outside all the limitations with which they had once identified. But most conscientious meditation masters know that to have this experience of detachment from one's past identity without proper preparation may well lead only to an extremely dangerous disarray. We may find ourselves without an identity at all, lost and unable to function. The successful escape from old entanglements may be made when a new identity has already been prepared, when at some level of conviction we have shaped a new ego, a new "I" (which may include the belief that we are not an individual self and have no ego). What really happens, then, may perhaps not be that we become "ego-less" but that we assume a new and wider selfhood, of whose boundaries we are unaware because they are so much broader or so much less confining than those of our old self. They may not, incidentally, be more true or valuable, but they are less uncomfortable for us.

The question we are asking is simply this: is any state of consciousness free from the formative influence of some expectation? There *may* even be a state of pathological withdrawal that is a complete rejection of all we had known, but is there a healthy mystical or meditative consciousness that is more than a focusing of our whole subjectivity upon a mind-set (or within a mind-set), a value identity that had already lain within us, even if not clearly recognized? Do we learn anything in an altered state of consciousness, or do we apprehend only a flavor, an orientation that we had already been shaping?

The importance of this question arises from the fact that if our experience is, after all, something other than "Truth-knowing-itself," if it is our being possessed by an orientation that had been prepared in us by teaching, by thinking, or by some other experience, then it is by no means self-authenticating and must submit to the criticism of alternative opinion. Govinda himself seems to recognize that our highest mystical states are in need of defense:

> One may object, that such visions are purely subjective and therefore nothing ultimate. However, words and ideas are nothing ultimate either. . . . The subjectivity of inner vision does not diminish its reality-value. Such visions are not hallucinations, because their reality is that of the human psyche.[16]

The philosophical critic must find Lama Govinda's statement rather unsatisfying. No one wishes to argue that words and ideas are "ultimate," and philosophers are always engaged in submitting them to the most rigorous examination they can manage. To defend mystical intuition on the ground that it is *as* ultimate as words and ideas, or at least that its lack of ultimacy is shared by them, seems rather beside the point. The last sentence in Govinda's remark is, of course, patently a statement of faith. As the eye cannot see the eye, the psyche cannot objectify and perceive itself. Therefore it is not possible to know either that a "vision" constitutes whatever we mean by the psyche or that it participates in the psyche's "reality." Even if the vision and the psyche did share the same reality (whatever that means) this would not prove that the vision was not somehow misshapen, for one presumes that a psyche may be awry in its functioning.

An altered state of consciousness is always impressive, simply because it is outside the regular pattern of our mental life. When it occurs within a framework of evaluation that exalts it and endows it with "ultimacy," we are likely to be overwhelmed by the seemingly incontrovertible significance of the experience and to accept fully, without serious question, the dogmas about it which the tradition has presented to us. Alas, this does not mean that even the noblest of our intuitions is more than a state of the individual mind, or that the most ancient and revered interpretive tradition is beyond question.

One feature of many meditationally induced states, however, that seems especially compelling is their holistic nature. Where our ordinary, linear thinking achieves understanding one step at a time, and then only imperfectly, the intuitive vision is complete and seems to apprehend the truth at once. The meditator feels that he or she has "arrived," has broken out of the miasma of illusion, has *seen* clearly and for the first time. It is useless to say "But you were set up for this; this is only your whole-minded and wholehearted centering on a quite questionable way of being." The joyful seer replies, "But before, I saw only fragments of the universe and its puzzling lack of meaning; now I see it all. Beyond words, beyond descriptions and definitions, what I see is simply ALL."

We have already argued that such an awareness, however convincing to the person who has it, is still only a state of mind as limited as the mind that holds it. Perhaps we can add a little to our critique if we approach from a slightly different angle.

When we read a novel that is genuinely a work of art, we become immersed in its "world." There comes a moment when, at least while we are actually reading the book, we enter into that world and it becomes ours. We apprehend it, so to speak, holistically. At last we put the book down and return to the world of our regular experience. But since the words used in the book are also the words we and others use about the "other" world of daily life, there is likely to be a relationship between the two worlds. We may feel that the novel has sharpened our grasp upon reality, that it has helped us to see things about life that had escaped us. We may even live a little differently, because the book has conditioned us to see our environment with "new" eyes.

Sometimes it happens that the world of the book and that of ordinary life are not compatible. The differences between them are so great that despite our involvement in the novel we cannot really relate what we "saw" there to what we "see" outside it. If this is so we usually, perhaps reluctantly, begin to think of the story as a fantasy, as unrealistic or "farfetched." Occasionally, however, someone prefers the unreal world to the real one, and begins to conduct himself or herself as if the imaginary were the true. When this happens, friends are likely to observe that our reader's behavior has become strange, eccentric, maybe even insane. The problem is that he or she is inhabiting one set of convictions with the mind, while acting in a world where they do not fully apply. The problem is *not* that he or she lacks an internally coherent or even holistic and compelling vision, but simply that the vision does not fit reality.

So it may happen that a personally satisfying, subjective experience is preferred by us to the more troublesome reality around us, and we may give ourselves with singleness of mind to it. We are likely to feel more powerful and more peaceful than ever before, and we may even appear "whole," saintly, charismatic, or divine to others. But our accomplishment is no more than a retreat into a conviction that satisfies, and whether its origin is a novel or a yogic trance it is equally vulnerable to the charge that it is a fabrication.

If, therefore, we choose to accept a vision of reality that is at odds with common experience, we should at least acknowledge that we have made a choice and that the acceptance of either "world" is in some degree an act of faith. Not to recognize this is by no means to escape from faith to fact, but from faith to fanaticism.

In summary, when someone regards a state of awareness as more than that—as, let us say, a perception of truth and reality—he or she is, consciously or otherwise, making a value judgment which the experience itself cannot justify. There are probably many factors at work in the decision, but among them will doubtless be the mind-set in which it was embedded and also the environing conditions, tradition, teaching, or other setting in which it occurred.

* * * * *

To this point we have tried to ask some questions about certain fairly common claims made for some altered states of consciousness. In doing so, we have taken those claims seriously but have refused to be intimidated by the aura of sanctity that sometimes surrounds them. Rasputin, after all, was endowed with something like sanctity in the eyes of a royal family, but he proved to be less than transcendentally wise. Many far more engaging characters than he may be quite as mistaken, and we must wonder whether the critical use of an intellect that has taken millennia to evolve is not the natural medicine with which alone we may try to cure or prevent our own illusions. Even Roberto Assagioli, to whom we referred in the last chapter, has discovered that intuition must be constrained by rational criticism, and the historic debates and denunciations among various mystics, gurus, and schools of meditation seem to confirm this judgment.

It is clear, from what we have said, that cold reason does not necessarily find much that is convincing about the sort of claims we have examined. Either they seem to be very questionable, or their significance is greatly diminished. In concluding this chapter, then, we may return to a question already briefly touched upon: why are these claims so enthusiastically embraced by some persons? It is true that a growing number of enthusiasts can be found who become, at last, disenchanted; but an impressive number of the faithful remain. What is so extraordinarily valuable about altered states of consciousness that people are willing to abandon a great deal and to undertake an entirely revised lifestyle in response to them?

What follows is not intended as a blanket denunciation of mystics or meditators but as an attempt to throw a little light on some of the statements spawned in the popular literature of the day.

Ontological Anxiety

To be self-conscious is to be aware of one's existence as more or less precarious. As soon as we know that we are not united by some invisible umbilical cord to the rest of the universe, we know that the universe may survive without us, and our delight in life is attended by some measure of anxiety about the possibility of losing it.

This natural, and not necessarily debilitating, concern for survival may grow acute if circumstances intensify in us a lack of confidence about our competence to live. Moreover, our anxiety tends to be compounded when our environment is too filled with change, confusing choices, and conflicting demands. When television bombards us nightly with commercials designed to stimulate our acquisitiveness so that we endure a state of chronic dissatisfaction with our lot, and when the newspaper confronts us every morning with a world of such rapid change, of such staggering ranges of possibility, of such dangers and perplexities as our time presents, it is little wonder that many grow weary and want only to simplify themselves and their lives. The attraction of the typical commercial guru is, then, easy to understand. He comes before us, as someone has aptly said, as the complete perma-press personality, able to resist wrinkles and always presentable, and he offers us insulation against the erosion of unfulfilled desire as well as a barricade against all the fears that haunt those who dare to face the world with their self-consciousness and finitude bravely nailed to the mast.

Norman Melchert correctly notes that "persons who seek unitive experience are typically persons profoundly dissatisfied with their lives as they have experienced them."[17] They are, consequently, in search of some remedy and are prepared to give themselves profoundly to anything that seems quite outside the range of options already familiar to them. "They hope desperately that there is some state more satisfactory than that of their own small self, with its hates and fears, its anxieties and burdens."[18]

It is inevitable that unitive experience or almost any significantly altered state of mind may appeal as the goal for which such persons have been searching. It is so richly different, so utterly peaceful yet triumphant, that it appeals at once as the fulfillment of our life, and to question its credentials or its place in the scheme of things seems crass, the mean business of a carping and trivial mind.

The haunted self finds self-forgetfulness, and gratefully chooses to believe it has actually leaped into its true character, leaving behind the old and painful illusion of finitude. We are, so the experience persuades us, not trembling on the brink of extinction, because we are more than we ever understood ourselves to be. The old finite ego was nothing, a vapor, a bauble to be cast aside now that it is discovered to be worthless. What *is* is found to be nothing less than the boundless, unassailable, pure consciousness which can know no enemy.

But one must ask why the person of whom we are speaking is so resistant to recognizing that his or her most remarkable state of consciousness is, after all, only a state of consciousness and the product of a still finite organism. Melchert writes: "If he were to say that this experience was merely an experience had by himself, the same individual person, nothing would fundamentally have been gained."[19] It is one's limit as an individual that he or she wants to surmount, it is the universal that he or she wants to find; so there is an almost irresistible motivation to identify one's experience of unity and wholeness with the inexpressible "Truth" of reality itself.

The philosopher who chooses to remain faithful to reason, however, must insist that we cannot assume a correspondence between *any* product of a human brain and a reality that is bigger than finitude. Indeed, such an assumption seems spontaneously self-discredited to those who do not share it but who observe the behavior of the person who does.

According to an old story, there was once an ostrich that stood upon a vast plain, almost in the center of a flock of other ostriches. Wherever it looked, there were birds of its own kind. At last it became desperately tired of their company and, to escape, our bird thrust its head into the sand and found there sweet privacy. After a few hours of this, the ostrich began again to want company, so it drew its head out of the sand and looked around. A strange thing had happened since it last looked, however; every single ostrich in the flock had meanwhile stuck *its* head in the sand. Slowly our hero looked around in every direction. A look of bewildered alarm crossed its face: "Where did they go?"

To the critical person, the claims of ontological significance that are commonly made for states of consciousness (claims that they disclose a truth about our "being") may seem no more valid than the assumptions of our ostrich. But to the person in a sufficiently uncomfortable state of anxiety about existence, the gap between the subjective experience of boundlessness and the facts of the universe is not obvious at all.

Identity Conflict

Closely related to this "ontological anxiety" is the problem faced by many modern people of establishing a coherent and consistent identity—a confident assurance of who and what they really are—and those having trouble with this may also be powerfully drawn to respond uncritically to some of the prevalent beliefs about certain dramatic modes of consciousness. This difficulty with identity is a fairly wide-spread problem today, and although it has been often analyzed, it deserves at least a brief examination here.

It is a common enough observation that ours is an age in which many persons struggle fruitlessly to achieve identity. This quest for identity is related to our growing failure to sustain more than casual and shallow relationships. Identity is both nourished by intimacy and is indispensable to the deepest forms of intimacy, since those who do not confidently know themselves cannot invest themselves wholeheartedly in an interest in others.

But what do we mean by "identity"?

Basing his thought on his investigations in psychology, one recent writer, William Kilpatrick, has said, "Identity is, first of all, a conviction of self-sameness—a bridge over the discontinuities which invariably creep or crash into our lives."[20] It is the assured recognition of oneself as that person who has endured through all the changes, the growths and diminishments, the triumphs and defeats of the years. This does not mean that identity is a static, rigid thing impervious to growth. On the contrary, it is really a process in which we are continually assimilating the new facts about ourselves without losing ourselves. It is, when healthy, a balance between sameness and newness, between continuity with the past and movement into the future. But it is also the confidence that the bundle of personal traits that are in a new configuration today is also the present moment of who you were yesterday.

There are at least five conditions necessary for the achievement of identity. We must have a sense of personal history, a sense of movement into a future that is ours, the experience of intimacy, the making of commitments and choices, and a certain amount of courage.

Speaking about personal history, Kilpatrick says that "a sure way to rob a person of identity is to take away his history. This loss of history explains the confusion of the amnesia victim, as well as the docility of the brainwashed prisoner."[21] A sense of having come from somewhere (to which, in some measure, we still belong—or, better, which still belongs to us) is essential to knowing who we are, and this is why the revolutionaries who want to change everything may be more complete in their identity than the generation that immediately follows their successful coup: they know whence they have come, and even in rejecting it they possess their past. If they are not careful, they will spawn a generation with no past and therefore also with no assurance of being anyone in particular. A totalitarian revolutionary, of course, is not alarmed by this, because persons who are no one in particular are ideal subjects of a projected new order. However, it is not unknown for the aftermath of effective revolution to see the rewriting of history so that people may be given a past which will build in them an identity acceptable to the regime.

But it is not enough to know ourselves as coming from somewhere; we must also have hope for the future. Soon after World War II, Viktor Frankl, a Viennese psychotherapist, founded a school of "logotherapy," based largely on the conviction that many neuroses are the result of inadequate philosophy or views about life's possible meanings. Describing his experiences in a Nazi concentration camp, Frankl showed that the persons who survived there were those who could continue to hope that at some time in the future their present suffering would acquire meaning.[22] While others were describing human beings as pleasure- or power-seeking animals, Frankl's experience led him to see us as persons who need the hope that the values for which we live will be fulfilled in the future.

There must also be intimacy. We must be confirmed as persons by others whom we engage in more than superficial relationship. There should be those around us who have shared with us some of our past and who affirm and confirm what and who we have been and are. New intimacies are important, too, since in each of them we see ourselves reflected and confirmed, and because they may lead us to define ourselves once more. It should be clear that "intimacy" has here no necessary sexual reference, but indicates a relation in which two persons address each other with openness and acceptance, really being "present" to each other with frankness and respect, concern and compassion.

But even a sense of past and future, and the confirmation of friends, may not quite give us that firm knowledge of ourselves that we are calling identity. We must add to these the experience of making commitments and choices. It is, in fact, out of these that our identity actually takes shape. In Kilpatrick's words, "It is through choice that an individual actually creates a self, and the ability to choose is essential to identity formation."[23]

Choice-making and commitment entail a saying "No" to some possibilities even in the very act of saying "Yes" to others. This is one place where courage is required of us, because no one can ever be quite sure that the lost possibilities may not have turned out to be better than those chosen. But not to choose is not to become anything; it is to remain amorphous and unactualized. Adam and Eve in the old story are given a tree from which they must not eat, and one may surmise that it is precisely the need to say "Yes" or "No" and thus to make a commitment that is being illustrated there. To make the wrong commitment alienates them from God, but alienation may be overcome. To make no choice at all is not to become real persons and is the greatest of all human calamities.

Courage is required also for intimacy. To be honest in our presentation of ourselves to others, really to be *there* for them, is always to risk rejection and injury. Yet even in being rejected we may, if we have already achieved enough self-confidence, learn something new about ourselves and even make strong our will to be faithful to ourselves.

It is difficult to achieve a perspective on one's own time, but it certainly seems to be true that identity is a more difficult achievement for us than for our grandparents. In the first place, we suffer from what Alvin Toffler has called "future shock." So many things are changing so rapidly that we tend to lose the feeling that the future will be recognizable and related to a present we understand. Such changefulness makes the attainment of a secure identity increasingly important, but also increasingly difficult.

Another ingredient in our present problem is the high mobility of many modern families, especially in the United States. This causes us to lack a place and a community in which we have grown up, a stable group of friends whose repeated friendly recognitions and whose participation in our past confirm us daily. Further, it is harder to make intimate friendships with a passing parade of persons than it is with those whose continuing proximity we can depend on.

Moreover, we are today confronted by a bewildering range of choices in education, work, pleasure, and environment. Choices are therefore more difficult to make, and when they are made they tend to be less definite than real commitments.

The result of all this is that many of us flounder in uncertainty about ourselves and are driven to seek comfort in identities that are too hastily or superficially constructed. The motorcycle gang with its uniform clothing, its ritualized behavior, and its delight in being feared is one such shallow identification. The impulse to carve or paint our names on rocks along the highway or even on the walls of rest rooms is similarly an indication of a hunger to be publicly recognized as someone.

Many contemporary theorists have argued for an abandonment of old-fashioned, firm identity in favor of fluidity. Commitment, it is argued, is confining; it is more comfortable to be "loose," with no options closed. Impulse rather than reasoned judgment seems usually to be espoused as the guide to action ("If it feels good, do it!"), and the present is emphasized as if it could be fulfilling without much reference to past or future. It is promised that when we rid ourselves of outworn roles and "binding expectations" concerning our own behavior or that of others, we shall relate more freely and fully than ever before.

Kilpatrick roundly attacks such a view. He says that the fluid lifestyle does lead to a sort of immediate and easy intimacy, but this should not be confused with authentic relationship. To *commune* with someone requires time, for deep relating develops almost like an organism. Quick intimacy smacks not of profound personal authenticity, but of emotional exhibitionism. Some recent studies of encounter groups seem to support this point of view, even when the researchers were inclined to favor the fluid process.[24]

> What is misleading is the currently popular view that deep and intense relationships can flourish in an uncluttered present. . . . A man who lived purely in the present would have the affectlessness of an amnesia victim.[25]

Perhaps it is worth noting that many of those authorities who most ardently recommend the indeterminate personality have themselves been the products of a long and very definite personality formation and can afford to be flexible because they do so on the ground of a clear personal identity.

Another device for dealing with our lack of identity is a turning to some "cult of simplicity." Among these we may find the unquestioning conformity and ecstatic religious experience of some kinds of the "Jesus movement," the Krishna cult, some communes, and other groups that provide a ready-made identity which we have simply to put on. This, of course, cripples personal growth and is a form of inauthenticity.

Finally, there is a retreat from the problem of identity which accounts, in part, for the enthusiasm some people feel for spectacular modes of consciousness.

When it is claimed that "cosmic consciousness" or *samādhi,* satori, and so on obliterates a purely worthless and false sense of self and brings us fully into an indivisible unity of all, we are relieved of the burden of patiently building individuality. Instead of personal identity we are led to believe in a kind of superidentity in which the treasure of the serious, valuable, but fragile otherness of each of us is stricken of worth. Too often this universal oneness amounts in practice to no more than a narcissism in which the world of splendid but confounding particulars has been domesticated so deviously that it is reduced to a mere extension of one's self.

To rise ecstatically into the "All" may be an experience in which we learn to recognize the profundity of the bond that joins us as well as the separate integrities that make each of us unique. But it may also be the embracing of a bad faith in which we turn away from the task of individuation.

Birth is always a venture marked by a certain amount of pain, and a return to the womb must always seem a desirable alternative to a baby who is just emerging into independent life. But something impels the baby forward and forces upon it the risk of recognizing itself as real. Always, however, the womb awaits. When Marshall McLuhan advocates a new "tribalism," and a hundred assorted "Masters" urge us to "drop the ego," we are likely, then, to breathe a sigh of relief that our impulse to escape ourselves has such authoritative support. And when the experiences they point to can be cultivated and understood in the terms they have provided, we seem to have confirmed their teaching. But there is good reason to question that teaching.

Why, then, do so many persons presumably endowed with a capacity for critical thought (which, by the way, need not be faithless thought but thought that recognizes faith for what it is) fail to ask pertinent questions or to see flaws in what they have been told? The answer is, I think, that we live in one of those periods when romanticism reigns supreme and intellectualism is despised, when there is a flight from reason. Reason demands its own discipline, and to sharpen it and use it well is not a simple task. Reason, it is said, has created many of our modern problems: its children are science and skeptical philosophy, and these have made our time perilous. Thus reason is often today made the lapdog of impulse and is used, if at all, merely to rationalize and justify whatever makes us comfortable.

Again, careful thought is always an individual responsibility, even when two or more persons do it together. It serves to make us aware of our separateness and our liability to error, and these can be very intimidating perceptions. Peter Berger says, "Man cannot accept aloneness and he cannot accept meaninglessness. The masochistic surrender [of individuality and our particular selfhood] is an attempt to escape aloneness by absorption in an other, who at the same time is posited as the only and absolute meaning."[26]

Thus a "spiritual experience" in which the self is lost in an Absolute is a protective masochism likely to be popular when the time is hazardous or confusing. A God who creates our particularity and demands of us that we try to fulfill it is apt to be less popular than a Cosmic Subjectivity that did not deliberately create us and in the light of which our selfhood can be viewed as a mistake.

But one of the simplest partial explanations of the fact that some altered states of consciousness are today so often taken to be Truth or Reality can be stated very succinctly: in rationalist eras God (or the "Ground of our being") tends to be reduced to an idea or concept; in romantic ones God is reduced to an experience. In both, the Creator is created in our image. The intriguing question remains whether anything that deserves to be called "God" (that is, anything that deserves to be loved with all our heart and soul and mind and strength) exists beyond ourselves.

6

The Future of an Illusion?

The last two chapters have raised some serious questions about the claims that are sometimes made for the significance of various states of our consciousness which may be achieved through meditation (or, perhaps, even through drugs). It may be convenient to summarize the most important of these and then go on to ask whether any beliefs, commitments, or convictions remain possible for us in the light of what has been said so far.

This is an important issue because it will be clear that some of our questions and reservations apply to *any* state of consciousness. Our interest in this short chapter, then, is the question: *when we have asked what we have now learned to ask about states of consciousness, what, if anything, remains to us as material for conviction, belief, or commitment?* Above all, is there now any possibility of *religious* conviction? Or was Freud correct in his little book whose title we have borrowed for this chapter: are religious ideas "illusions" demonstrably discredited and due to be discarded in favor of a more "rational" approach to life?

A Summary of Our Questions

If we look back over the last two chapters we will find that the inquiries or criticisms contained in them may roughly be reduced to three kinds. First, we have asked in several ways, "Are you sure your so-called higher state of consciousness was all that it seemed to you to be? Could it, instead, be no more than your reentry into a forgotten prenatal state of mind or into that pre-verbal one which you must have had soon after birth? Is it, perhaps, a misleading withdrawal of your energies and attention from everything that lies outside you and a focusing of them on your own subjectivity—in short, no more than pure narcissism?"

Again, can we defend the hope that meditative experience is more than simply a change from one to the other of the "bimodal" functions of the brain? Is the sense of liberation from a false self, which many enjoy in meditation, no more than release from old habits of thought and belief without necessarily being also an entry into "truth" about ourselves?

This first array of questions asks whether we can depend without doubt on the belief that the most remarkable alteration of our mind is more than the result of a very mundane electrochemical process that really has no truth-value and requires for its explanation no reference to anything more cosmic than molecules and energy.

Our next set of questions concerns not so much the nature of the experience as its interpretation. What is the meaning, significance, or value of the altered consciousness? Can any new "understanding" or "vision" that comes to us through meditation ever be beyond doubt, ever be self-confirming? Following Kant's lead, we have asked whether it is possible to infer something about a person's status in the universe by examining his or her state of mind, and we have seen that there is no necessary connection between infinitude as a form of consciousness and actual infinitude. Obviously, if we experience some extraordinary mental state, we may allow it to suggest a hypothesis about our existence, but we have found no reason to let it seem to guarantee any conclusion we may be led to draw about that existence.

A mounting body of evidence suggests that our prior (even unrecognized) assumptions and our method of meditation itself may both influence the result, so that what seems at first to be a clear, unmediated, spontaneous "breakthrough" into "truth" may be no more than the result of a successful process of conditioning the mind. This means that the most convincing of conscious states is no spontaneous appearance of naked truth, and whatever it seems to disclose about reality must be subjected to careful, rational criticism. It may seem transparently clear, for example, that the world of things and persons around us is really a construction of our imagination; but we must allow ourselves to ask whether it is not more likely that our imagination is a construct of the world of things around us! Does an actual world evoke our mind's awareness of it, or does our mind create the image of a world? This issue cannot be settled by any special attainment of consciousness, not even one which has expunged awareness of the world.

A third line of inquiry concerns the motivation for belief. Does it make a difference to the strength of our conviction if we are forced to recognize that we enjoy holding it because it meets a profound need in us? Perhaps it dispels our dread of death, of finitude, of loss, or of lack of identity; it may help us rise above our sense of vulnerability to others or to impersonal, crass circumstance; it may remove our fear of uncertainty, our insecurity in the face of a world that offers us more questions than answers. Should we be distrustful of any conviction that we find to be satisfying?

Here, then, are three fairly typical statements intended to question claims for the truth-value of altered states:

(1) A state of consciousness is *only* that, and gives us no ground whatever for unquestioning belief about its content or apparent implications.

(2) A conviction that flatters or reassures us is very likely to be wrong, however persuasive it may seem. If we spontaneously enjoy a belief, it is likely to be hazardous to our sanity!

(3) Subjectivist or idealist views of "truth" or "reality" are always especially dubious because they appeal strongly to our pride or our longing for a security which depends on nothing outside our "real" self (even the notion of losing the self is a very self-satisfying thing!). Further, such beliefs render the world harmless, but by falsifying our relation to it, by making the world a mere figment of our thought. Meditation usually produces or tends to confirm such subjectivist disvaluing of the world's otherness, and is therefore an archenemy not only of truth, but of realism, empiricism, common sense, and courage.

Some of our questions strike at the heart not only of meditative states, but of *all* states of mind—or, rather, of any conclusions about reality that we might draw from them. If we take such questions and reservations seriously, can we believe *anything*? Is not a conviction, belief, or even an act of knowing *always* and necessarily a "state of consciousness" and therefore, according to our critique, "dubious"?

Are we left with not only skepticism about certain exotic altered states of consciousness, and the beliefs or alleged "knowledge" that some would claim as a result of them, but a complete skepticism about all knowing and all belief? On the other hand, if we find it possible to believe *anything*, must we necessarily believe *everything*?

A Constructive Response

There is, indeed, no good reason for denying that the electrical, chemical, or other purely natural operations of a physical organism, a matter-energy system, is responsible for states of mind. Destroy the organism, and its thinking or meditative experience stops. Alter the physical form of a brain, and thinking or intuiting is also altered. This means that all subjective states are dependent on the physical apparatus of our bodies.

But this does not mean that an idea, a conviction, or a perception is no more than an electrochemical event. To argue that because it is such an event it is *only* that is to commit the grossest of logical blunders: it is to identify the process and the product, almost as if we were to say that a Rolls Royce *were* the Rolls Royce factory. While refusing, then, to call in some supernatural source for our forms of consciousness, we also refuse to discredit the *possibility* that they actually disclose truths that are beyond the process of our brains.

Very well, but is there any way to guarantee the objective, inevitable, absolutely reliable certainty of any of our ideas? We may feel reasonably sure that we have really just experienced the condition called *satori* in Zen or *samādhi* in many traditions; but how certain is our idea that this condition meant something, that it signified something beyond the fact that the human central nervous system is capable of such an experience?

Alas, the answer to this must be that it is not very certain at all. We have an experience of a certain striking sort; we interpret it in a certain way, and ideas about it arise; subjectivity takes many shapes— these are simple facts, and can be questioned as facts only by those who are willing to deny that their questioning itself is an experience, idea, and subjective state. But the validity of any of our conclusions, the truthfulness of any idea, the meaning we give to any state of consciousness is always and unavoidably questionable.

I perceive myself as sitting at a typewriter and writing these words. I feel fairly confident that the typewriter, the typing, and the typist are real enough. But I cannot possibly "prove" that they are! It is possible that the entire world is, after all, a figment of imagination. And it is just as possible that any experience I may have that seems to prove or establish some other view of things is spurious—or that what it suggests to me about life is no more than a peculiar aberration of my brain.

The great Buddhist, Nagarjuna, might say to me: "I have discredited every concept and have achieved a state of mind that cannot be described. It is free of ideas, devoid of impressions. It is not to be called either consciousness or unconsciousness, existence or non-existence." To this I might respond politely that such must be a quite remarkable moment. But if Nagarjuna goes on to suggest that there is some further value to the experience, I am not obliged to follow him. I know something of why he may like to value it as he does, of what constructs subjectivity, and I know that no conclusion, no conviction, no understanding is unquestionable, not even the "convictionless conviction" that All is Empty!

To put the matter bluntly, I know nothing that *must* be true, and neither does Nagarjuna.

Well, then, am I cast adrift in a world of meaninglessness? Must I have no beliefs at all? Is conviction impossible?

This question has haunted intelligent and critical people for thousands of years—at least since Socrates; and his handling of the situation may be a good place for us to begin to find an answer.

Heuristic Commitment: A Socratic Solution

Throughout Plato's dialogues we are presented with a picture of Socrates as a man dedicated to inquiry. He rigorously examines ideas and propositions in order to find the most appropriate direction for his life. But at no point is he shown to us as one who achieves or expects to achieve in this life a final certitude about anything. His life, one may almost say, is his continuing inquiry, and his inquiry constantly appraises his life. The one thing he claims to know with certainty is that he knows nothing of importance. Even at the most critical moment of his public life, in the *Apology* he is shown defending himself against various accusations, but remaining adamant that he is a seeker, not a holder, of any inviolable truth.

One might expect such a man to be ridden with insecurity, to be incapable of decisive action, to be without any firm conviction at all. But Socrates defies our expectation. In all the dialogues he is represented as displaying a vigorous and unusually cheerful mind, committed to certain courses of action. And nowhere is this more impressive than in the *Crito*, Plato's poignant story of Socrates' refusal to accept the means of escape that his friends want to obtain for him.

With the aid of his colleague, Crito, Socrates reviews some of his own cherished opinions, calls in question the very bases on which he has lived the life that has brought him under sentence of death, and then staunchly sets his face to continue on his present course. Has he achieved certitude about his opinions and convictions? Not at all. He has only found that the beliefs that led him to his trial and sentence are unshaken by argument: they still conform to his best reason and experience, and therefore he will follow them to the end.

What Socrates is displaying might be called "heuristic commitment." The adjective "heuristic" is, like Archimedes' famous cry "Eureka!", derived from the Greek word *heuriskein,* meaning to discover, to observe, to recognize as feasible. Anything that is believed heuristically is believed as part of a continuing journey of exploration and therefore is open to a new and contradictory discovery tomorrow. It is the best idea or conviction we have so far discovered, making sense of all our experience, but it is not clutched dogmatically as if it must never again be exposed to inquiry. "Heuristic commitment" is, therefore, a commitment to act upon what we have so far discovered to be satisfactory after critical thought, with the realization that we may some day have to change our minds.

The issue that Socrates' life raises is the enormous difference between heurism and the lust for certainty. Probably few of us can stand to entertain uncertainty in all areas of our lives at once, and the result is that when we turn to a consideration of something as important for the very foundation of our living as religion, we hunger for absolute and unquestionable confidence. So we may give up our reason to some "master" who will tell us what to believe. We may follow the Reverend Bob Jones to suicide in Guiana or we may clutch the words of a sacred text as if no thought needed to be used on it. In Dostoevsky's famous "Grand Inquisitor" chapter of the novel *The Brothers Karamazov*, the inquisitor appeals to the masses by telling them what to believe, and rightly accuses Jesus of burdening them with the unwelcome responsibility of thinking for themselves and making heuristic commitment. Most of us are more comfortable with the Inquisitor!

But the sort of certitude we seek is simply not available to finite human beings. This does not mean, however, that we cannot hold a conviction with a high degree of confidence. It means that our convictions must always be matters of faith, and faith is distinguished from fanaticism by its awareness that it is not final and unquestionable knowledge. Faith is opposed to all versions of what we may call fundamentalism—not only the fundamentalism of a book (whether the Bible, the Koran, or some other Scripture) but the fundamentalism of personal experience as well. There is even a fundamentalism of skeptical reason—the unquestioned conviction that to have shown that something is unproven is to have shown that it is wrong. Heuristic conviction, or faith, is never fanatical but is perfectly capable of great strength and decisive action.

So we return to our first question of this chapter. Are the questions and objections we have raised necessarily the death-knell of meditation's truth-claims in particular or of religious commitment in general?

No. But the brave and honest spirit will pursue the inquiries we have raised and will reach heuristic conclusions that seem, at the moment, to make the best sense of his or her experience.

After this series of explanations that raise questions we ought to take seriously, we may still feel that some religious interpretation of life is not only possible, but is the most reasonable and productive we can attain. Faith is required for the holding of such an interpretation, and even braver faith for living its implications; but faith is required for all important human ventures, including science (where we must have faith that there is a world to study, that we can apprehend important elements of it with our instruments, that data shared by other investigators is reliable, and so on). Faith is required even for such daily adventures as marriage and eating in restaurants.

For some, then, we may presume that the conclusions about altered states of consciousness will remain matters of conviction—we hope, heuristic conviction. Recognizing that no alternative religious commitment can escape the demand to be heuristic, we may now go on to ask: is it possible to participate in a religious orientation to life and yet find reasons to add further questions to those we have already considered about the truth-claims of meditative states?

The answer is that it evidently is, and we must move on to examine a little of the content of one sample alternative and the doubts it may express about some aspects of meditation. The alternative of Christianity is a powerful tradition in our culture, and many are unaware of its unique perspective toward our subject.

7

Theological Reflection

We always see things from some particular vantage point. Every amateur photographer knows the chagrin of seeing a picture that is much better than his or her own because its owner found a better angle, a more interesting perspective. I have never met a person whose viewing of life did not also betray a point of view, an angle, although there have been many who thought they had achieved "presuppositionless thinking" or "pure perception." The problem is that, when it is a matter of our understanding of ourselves and of life, our perspective is so much a part of us that we easily fail to recognize its existence.

In ancient India many persons believed that there was no permanent, unchanging "self" in us, no "soul" that exists eternally. Led by the Buddha, they saw that what we usually call our "self" is more like a set of functions than a "thing" or being which *performs* functions. As they examined the way our psyches work, their perspective led them to interpret what they saw as a flow or flux with nothing enduring within it or supporting it. On the other hand, many other persons (such as the eminent Vedantist, Sankara) saw the same data from a different perspective. Of course we experience our existence as a flow, and a constant process of change. But can an infinite series of changes really be regarded as self-explanatory? Certainly not. Therefore there is "Something" that underlies the change and is itself enduringly the same. Sankara's perspective led him to see as self-evident the "truth" that this

"Something" is perfect, and being perfect is actually *un*changing. Therefore the "real" does not change, and change must be somehow less than real!

Both the Buddha and Sankara would claim to have attained the highest degree of spiritual insight, the highest condition of consciousness, the clearest knowing. Yet they disagree about what their knowing means. Each has a perspective so pervasive and subtle that he himself does not recognize its presence and assumes that he simply "knows." And each feels his vision to be self-authenticating and beyond question.

None of us, then, escapes the limits of perspective, and this makes communication between persons both more difficult and more necessary. Further, it makes the acceptance of the fact of faith indispensable to reasonable discourse. Our option is not, as is sometimes naïvely supposed, between faith and reason, or between faith and direct experience, but between faith and fanaticism. Faith knows that it is the acceptance of and trust in a perspective; fanaticism does not. Faith can therefore question its own perspective and attempt to explore others. It is the ground on which all genuine dialogue can proceed. Fanaticism precludes dialogue and insists on conversion of the other (a very curious situation, incidentally, when the fanaticism also denies that "otherness" is real!).

What, then, is a Christian perspective? This question has no simple answer, for it must be clear that an almost infinite variety of opinions on important subjects confronts the inquirer who wants to find *the* Christian view. In what follows, however, it will be assumed that Christian theology begins as reflection on the significance for the world of a particular historical person understood in a particular way. The person is, of course, Jesus of Nazareth, and the understanding entails the view that in hin occurred a unique and decisive action of God, an action that has forever provided us with a sort of North Star by which our lives may be directed toward fulfillment and meaning. In general, Christians have agreed to understand the world and their place in it from the perspective that emerges as a result of their listening to the message of Jesus.

This means that Christianity is not a prefabricated metaphysics or science. Rather, the Christian says to the metaphysician and scientist, "Show me what the universe is like and I'll try to tell you what it means that the Christ has happened in it."

It is true, however, that a great many opinions have been elevated by Christians to the status of revelation. In a recent, and very illuminating, work on the psychobiology of mind, William R. Uttal states, "This approach contends that the mind and the body are related in such a basic manner that without the body, the mind does not exist."[1] This means that instead of consciousness being the foundational reality that somehow causes at least the appearance of a physical world, the reverse is in fact true: it is the physical, the material, the organic that is the cause of mind. Mr. Uttal then remarks that this premise "conflicts in a fundamental way with the predominant theologies of our society."[2]

Unfortunately, Uttal is correct about our theologies. Yet the truth is that it is only by a distortion of Jewish or early Christian understanding that these systems of thought can be made unacceptant of his premise. The psychobiological view of the mind-body relationship that he espouses can be said to have been roughly normative for the writers of the Bible. The Old Testament, for example, is remarkably free of preoccupation with the survival of our consciousnesses beyond physical death, and despite occasional hints to the contrary generally regards death as a termination of our relationship even with God. In the New Testament we find the surprised and joyful proclamation that Christ has risen—that God has shown that death is not the goal of life or its necessary defeat, and that even we may share in life's victory. But how? Even the usually undaunted speculations of Saint Paul flounder noticeably here. He simply cannot conceive of a "soul" that could exist without a body, of a consciousness that floated freely without a brain to produce it. Whatever may be the case with God (and that is a subject beyond useful speculation), with *us* survival of our own death could *only* mean some kind of bodily resurrection. Not that we need be supposed to have to face the reconstruction of a body exactly like the one we have worn out, but some kind of body we surely must have. Disembodied spirits were no part of early Christian thought. But Christians are open to the discovery that life and consciousness have *any* kind of basis. Their perspective insists only on the triumph of life.

The point we are making is that Christianity must not be understood as a finished philosophy, committed to some very specific world-view. Rather it is a commitment, a listening, and a perspective. Christians seem to themselves to have been grasped by an action of God so that a particular point in history has become the compass point by which they direct their understanding, assimilate new data, and govern their life-motion toward wholeness. By this historical moment and this perspective they analyze every claim of enlightenment, but they know that what they have been given is a perspective, not a "seeing" that is devoid of the possibility of error.[3]

Yet this perspective is not entirely vacant of content. It does seem to favor one side over others in certain questions, and this is where it may lead a Christian to be critical of some of the conclusions that are occasionally drawn concerning extraordinary states of consciousness.

Self and Other

One of the most persistent questions of philosophy concerns the relation of the self (the person doing the thinking, experiencing, observing, and so on) and the other (that which is experienced, observed, known). Most of us live our daily lives as if there were no problem at all about this. We take for granted that everything and everyone we encounter is just as real as ourselves and that we are unquestionably real. However, nothing is allowed by philosophy to remain as uncomplicated as that!

We have already seen that many people have argued that there is "really" only subjectivity and that the appearance of "objects" is a construction of mind. This means that trees, cars, houses, and persons have a status something like ideas and dreams. If one goes this far it is usual to take the further step and to argue that there is only *one* mind, or consciousness, of which everything is a product. This means that while, at the level of reality-unreality in which we conduct our affairs we seem to relate to other persons and things, the *real* subject (or thinker, knower, experiencer) has no relations at all. There is just the thought or knowing or experiencing. Indeed, perhaps there is not even a think*er* or experienc*er*, but only thought or experience.

In any case, this line of understanding (or misunderstanding) leads as a rule toward what is called non-dualism or monism: the affirmation that "all is One."

A popular alternative to our non-dualism is pluralism. This is the view that many things are "real" and that many subjects or knowers exist independently of each other. When the non-dualist gently points out that he or she has attained a mental condition in which all otherness has vanished, that he or she has pierced the screen of illusion and has known the indivisible pure consciousness, the pluralist acidly remarks that a lot of people have done the same—and that is the point: the experience of non-duality does not establish the truthfulness of non-duality as a philosophy. From the pluralistic point of view, two mystics, sitting side by side, both experiencing non-duality are *really* a duality!

Christianity tries to steer a course between these extremes. It wants to take both plurality and oneness seriously. It is obliged to do this because its perspective is based on the Christ-event, the Universal Reality itself (or God) which has stood and walked among us in the existence of a certain person. This strange event is seen therefore as at once the affirmation of Universality (God is All) and of particularity (Jesus is envalued and endorsed as a singular, real, unrepeatable person, and therefore every singular person is envalued).

God, to put the matter shortly, is That in whom we live and move and exist, as Acts 17:28 puts it, but God is a *christing* One, which means that every particular individual in existence (now or at any time) is made valuable. *A christing God values, seeks, restores, heals, and loves every single person in every single moment of every single planetary system.*

This means that as this "self" which I both am and am becoming, I meet others who are equally real selves. All of us have our existence only within and by reason of God's power to *be*, but God's being or reality includes within it otherness as well as sameness, distance as well as nearness, strangeness as well as identity. This is the point which both the simple monist and the simple pluralist have failed to understand. All *is* "One," as the monist says: but that One is God in whom all particularity has its eternally envalued existence.

The Christ is precisely the proclamation of this perspective.

This is why he is not like an "avatar" of Vishnu, such as Krishna. Vishnu, like the various Greek and other ancient gods whom he resembles, is a deity who may become incarnate a number of times. The Christ is a once-for-all event. It can happen only once within any world's history, for it is the decisive and concrete proclamation that Oneness and manyness are both facets of the truth about us all. If this Christ-event occurred more than once, its word about the value of particularity, of every single person and event, of the unrepeated moment, would be lost. If it were perceived as merely another prophetic figure, like Moses or Isaiah, then it might say something useful about the value of particular individuality but not about oneness, for it would not be the presence of God. The Christian perspective has always seen that the all-embracing, ultimately unifying inclusiveness of God assures the serious reality of each individual, and that our lives must somehow express both these things. That is why Jesus taught that the greatest of all our human obligations is to love God with all our heart and mind and soul and strength, and that our second obligation is similar: it is to love our neighbor as ourselves. Here, expressed as ethical norm, is the same perspective: Allness and unique particularity, both as real, the one within the other.

This way of looking at our human condition suggests that we are in a rather odd situation. We cannot be separated ontologically (in respect of our *being*, our sheer "*isness*") from God, and therefore we belong to each other as members of a kind of continuum of being. Yet, since otherness exists within that continuum (within God), we are perfectly capable of being estranged from each other, and from that One who is the embracing All that includes us. We can be alienated, hostile, even vicious; but we cannot exist outside that One in whom all others are equally gathered.

This means that while the cosmos exists within God, God transcends it, embracing all its positive elements and all that negates it, all existence and all distance and space that separate existents.

Similarly, our consciousness and experience exist within God, but God transcends them. Even when our experience appears to us as boundless, a consciousness that is unlimited by any awareness of anything, it is still *our* consciousness and exists within God but not *as* God.

History becomes important because our actions exist within God but are not God. What we do really makes a difference, because difference can occur within God who is the reality of distance, distinction, motion, change, and all else that exists. Yet God, transcending our history, can take the rough stuff of our behavior and weave of it a final tapestry that expresses and fulfills Divinity itself.

The main point of this section is simple, but vital to a Christian appraisal of states of consciousness. As consciousness may be dependent on a brain, but is not exactly a brain, so in a larger sense the Christian thinks that brains and their consciousness are dependent on God, exist within God, arise as God's progressive self-expression, but are decidedly *not* to be identified with God. Already, then, we see that the Christian awakening to God's christing character makes us critical of the opinion that any state of awareness annuls our individuality or trivializes it. Each of us is irreducibly a single person, even while existing within God's field of being. We may worship either God or our own consciousness, but these are by no means the same worship. We have been called to individual existence within the universal "being" of God: to worship God is to foster one another's individuality without losing the awareness of the common divine Ground uniting us all.

Self-fulfillment or Self-abnegation

A recurrent refrain of unitive mysticism is the necessity for us to cast off the ego, to abandon the self. Now, Christianity often enough speaks in similar terms, but its meaning is usually significantly different. The Christian speaks about being "born anew" or "born from above" to indicate the nature of the experience he or she is advocating, and this should suggest immediately that it is an experience of becoming a new and different person rather than simply one of losing something. To put it plainly, the Christian faith is concerned with fulfillment of a person, not with the loss of what is usually meant by the self or ego.

This point becomes clear if we consider one of the central texts in the New Testament concerning the "denial" of self. Matthew, Mark, and Luke all report, in almost identical words, a saying of Jesus which indicates clearly that the denial of self he prescribes is to be achieved by (and is also for the purpose of) the devoting of ourselves to what he represents. In other words, *it is through an appropriate loyalty which evokes active, self-forgetting service that we are made whole.*

The text is, in Matthew's version,

> Then Jesus told his disciples, "If any man would come after me, let him deny himself and take up his cross and follow me. For whoever would save his life will lose it, and whoever loses his life for my sake will find it." (Matt. 16:24–25)

Thus it is "losing" oneself in loyalty to Christ, in "following" his path, that we are made whole. No time is wasted here in acts designed to "drop the ego," because they would reflect that "saving his life" by which a person becomes lost. The concern is not with losing something but with becoming something, with finding fulfillment through a supreme commitment.

This does not mean that there is nothing in common between the mystic "loss of ego" experience and the Christian "self-denying loyalty." We have already described the former as a stepping out of the cluster of hopes, values, fears, assumptions, and attitudes that normally make up the major content of what should probably really be called our superego. There is a sense of profound liberation, of having become boundless and authentic. Now, this emptying ourselves of old content in a sense of new freedom is likely to be part of what the Christian prizes as "new birth," but it is by no means all of it. Indeed, this stage in the process is not itself the "birth" at all but only the preliminary movement, for the culmination of the event is our becoming a new self with new content. It should be noted, moreover, that this rebirth may not happen suddenly or dramatically, but so gradually as the Christian's loyalty to Christ deepens that the loss of old values and attitudes and the adoption of new ones is scarcely observed.

In any case, the mere stepping back from old encrustations is an incomplete liberation, and unless a new value-orientation is available for us we may suffer a time of confusion and emptiness. Consider once more the curious allegory used by Jesus in the eleventh chapter of Luke's Gospel. A certain person has been set free from an "unclean spirit" and is consequently vacant as a personality. In time, since nothing takes the place of the evicted "spirit," it returns to repossess its old home. Finding everything there so beautifully empty, the "spirit" is encouraged to invite seven others of its kind who are even more malevolent than itself to share the dwelling (Luke 11:25–26)! The point of this is that, in a similar way, the "loss of self" does not perfect us, but merely sets us free from old loyalties and makes us available for new ones. Only in some new commitment do we become finally free from the old, and become an authentically new and "whole" person. Often, of course, the new allegiance is undertaken in the same moment the old is abandoned (this seems to be the classic pattern in all forms of "conversion"); at other times it is only the loss of the old that we perceive.

If we really are merely emptied of all old meanings, commitments, and values, then far from being free we are simply a vacuum into which anything might come. It is not uncommon for us to meet someone who has, with a feeling of real relief, thrown out the norms, rules, and beliefs of his or her parents. Feeling oppressed by them, perhaps bewildered by a too complicated culture, such a person may joyfully cast aside the family's religion or even "Western Civilization" or "the American Way of Life." These persons are, like the man in Jesus' parable, "swept clean" but quite vacant. Their danger is that they may be filled with something else no better than they had before but quite uncritically accepted. Thus in place of a Judaism or a Christianity that had become conventional, secondhand, and poorly understood, there is an enthusiastic scientism or occultism or something else, felt as marvelously "real" and "true" because it is held with the whole heart instead of being resisted, as was the forsaken system.

Christians are interested in what we become, not simply in what we abandon. Our life is focused in loyalties, and we seek a loyalty which does not diminish our authenticity but which draws us together into a wholeness, a coherent and reasonably consistent selfhood. We want not merely to be liberated from the old, but to be born anew in a higher measure of whatever truly fulfills our potential as human beings.

Further, Christians may be skeptical about the very sense of boundlessness, of unity with all Reality, of which some mystics and others speak. We do not doubt the reality of the experience, but we question it as an experience of reality. We know that in some cases the impression of having obliterated a limited self and having attained universality is really a mistaken perception of something quite different: of the expansion of the individual's self-consciousness until it has "absorbed" the cosmos and is unable to recognize otherness or limitation anywhere. The story of the Tower of Babel in the eleventh chapter of Genesis is a delightful warning against this sort of proud imperialism.

Even aside from such crude and illusory egoism, however, there are experiences in which all duality is lost to view and all boundaries seem to dissolve, but which are nevertheless not the ultimate attainment that many who enjoy them believe them to be. The eminent Jewish philosopher, Martin Buber, was one who experienced unitive mystical depth and who wrote espousing it, yet who finally came to see that this was properly only a stage in an unfinished pilgrimage, and that it was actually a kind of idolatry if taken to be fulfillment of our human destiny.

Buber argues that many persons make a mistake which had also been his. They manage to concentrate all the forces of their awareness, to withdraw them from whatever, outside the self, might distract them. At last a consciousness is attained that is without objects and is felt as whole and undefiled. This, says Buber, is an important and valuable achievement. But it can be mistaken for a *cosmic* unity when it is really only a unifying of the single consciousness of the person. Properly understood it is a prelude to the most momentous experience we may have: "Concentrated into a unity, a human being can proceed to his encounter—wholly successful only now—with mystery and perfection. But he can also savor the bliss of his unity and, without incurring the supreme duty, return into distraction."[4]

What Buber is saying is that the unification of the self, the concentrating and purging of our consciousness, is useful if it is done for the sake of our launching out into genuine encounter with real otherness—other things, other persons, and, through these, the irreducible and supreme Otherness that is God. But if we are content with our sense of inner unification we will fail to fulfill the obligation that birth into a world of others has imposed upon us, and thus we will fail to find the God who has created that world and is concealed within it. "All doctrines of immersion [that is, of undifferentiated oneness as our final truth] are based on the gigantic delusion of a human spirit bent back into itself."[5]

The Christian also believes that the true, creative God meets us in everything and everyone who confronts us and is not fully to be known through our turning into ourselves. What may distinguish a Christian from Martin Buber is the conviction that God has acted to endorse the importance of the single one, and has concretely demonstrated the essential character of healing relationship in Jesus when he confronts us as our Christ. The importance of this idea lies in the fact that without such a concrete instance of the presence of God in the world, we are left with only a philosophy of the divine, and philosophies are insufficient because they are dependent on words. In the Christ we have a personal event who can be engrossingly met but never satisfactorily accommodated in words. He is therefore the divine Word beyond words.

To what, then, does this Christ-Word invite us? Not to introversion or to any condition of pure consciousness alone, but to genuine meeting, to authentic relating, to *caring* for others (other things as well as other persons). The journey to God does not take us away from awareness of the world, but into it:

> . . . in truth, there is no God-seeking because there is nothing where one could not find him. How foolish and hopeless must one be to leave one's way of life to seek God: even if one gained all the wisdom of solitude and all the power of concentration, one would miss him.[6]

Further, the encounter with God, mediated through our openness to others and, so the Christian believes, preeminently through our encounter with the Christ and his concern for the world, is not designed to cancel our individuality, but by lifting us out of our preoccupation with ourselves, to sharpen it and to perfect us as persons. As Jesus is reported to have said, "For whoever would save his life will lose it; and whoever loses his life for my sake, he will save it" (Luke 9:24).

For the Christian, then, even a concern for one's own spiritual perfection is a form of self-centeredness, and a unitive state of consciousness is of use only as a clearing of the decks before we renew our wholehearted relationship with God and the world. The road to our destiny is the forgetting of ourselves in a loyalty so complete that our "self" takes shape without our concern for it.

The ego is a fragile thing, a mere function of relating to the world, and it is governed by whatever set of values we have adopted. Thus it is changeable and insubstantial, a thing of moments. But the *person* is both what we deeply are and what we are always becoming. It is our lifelong project, and the Christian has been led to nourish it not upon his or her own subjectivity, but upon Christ as a paradigm of the proper way to be human in this world. More than this, in the Christ he or she has seen God's eternal reaching to heal all creatures, and it has thus become clear that no amount of "spiritual" discipline can do what needs to be done. What we need above all else is simply the grateful acceptance of the relationship God has already offered.

Indeed, a grave danger of all "spiritual" attainments is that they may blind us to our need for that which they cannot provide. In Luke's eighteenth chapter there is the familiar story of the young man who asked Jesus what must be done to win eternal life—which means the fullness and perfection of life. Jesus confirmed that this man had been faithful to his religious tradition, and then advised him to give away his considerable wealth and become a disciple. The man, we are told, was unwilling to sacrifice what he had accumulated and went sadly away.

I think we must understand that it is not only financial wealth that precludes our having the humility and readiness to accept God. Intellectual and spiritual attainment may also be too much for us to put aside. But the discomforting word of the gospel is that nothing we have or can do will perfect our lives as persons until we have first acknowledged our profound and incurable poverty and have accepted what God freely offers—restored relationship with the Divine. It is the free availability of that relation that is meant by the old theological term "grace," and our unpretentious acceptance of this is the single critical business of our life, the one thing that really puts us on the path to fulfillment. Jesus once likened the spiritual leaders of his day to "white-washed tombs" (Matt. 23:27), meaning that they had concealed from themselves and others the corruption within, but had not removed it. The incomparable G. K. Chesterton has Father Brown astutely remark (in complete consistency with the spirit of the Gospels), "Frankly, I don't care for spiritual powers much myself. I've got much more sympathy with spiritual weaknesses."[7] It is our awareness of spiritual weakness that leaves room in us for God's coming; our sensitivity to our own attainment often obstructs God's entry.

Joseph Goldstein tells us that "someone once asked Trungpa Rinpoche where 'grace' fit into the Buddhist tradition. He replied that grace is patience. If we have a patient mind, all things will unfold in a natural and organic way."[8] This the Christian must regard as a capital error. What unfolds through patience is no more than what the organism has within it to begin with. Grace is the word for that coming to us by God that we cannot force, because God is more than our inwardness. In living toward God and thoroughly in the world through which God meets us, we find grace leading us toward the fulfilling of our created personhood.

Mysticism without grace is simply Titanism. A Titan may well be tranquil, feeling whole and one with the cosmos; but he or she is no more than a Titan nevertheless, possessed of a full measure of the vice of *hubris* even when that *hubris* is a pride so full and perfect that it appears as its very opposite, humility and selflessness.

The Imperative of Love

Claudio Naranjo has shown that detachment is not only a classic requisite of many oriental religions, but that it is integral to Christianity too. He says that detachment "is the marrow of the Christian repudiation of 'the world,' "[9] and supports this view by referring to *The Encyclopedia of Biblical Quotations* where the entry "world" receives, he reports, only negative pronouncements.

Here is a root of much confusion. Evidently the *Encyclopedia* failed to list the most famous text in the New Testament, John 3:16, where we are told that "God so loved the world. . . ." The fact is that the biblical attitude to the world about us was a great deal more appreciative than centuries of infiltration by hellenistic and oriental opinion might suggest. Even for Saint Paul it is not merely humanity but the entire universe that is "created through [Christ] and for him" (Col. 1:16), and it is the "whole creation . . . groaning in travail" (Rom. 8:22) that waits for the consummation of God's good intention for it.

The Christian, then, is not withdrawn from the world but made able to look at it and live in it in a new way.

The essence of that new way is love. In its few pages the New Testament is chiefly concerned with extolling that love between *persons*, and in doing so it indicates that Jesus taught that the indispensable essence of the old Hebrew law was first to love God with all our being, and second to love our neighbor as ourselves (Luke 10:25–28). Nor is our "neighbor" simply the friendly fellow who lives next door— or his wife. Luke 6:28 says we are to love even our enemies!

This command to love is really very difficult, especially if we take the otherness of our enemy seriously. But it is a *command*—that is, a directive for adequate living, because it is in whatever is meant here by "love" that we are finally delivered from diseased self-preoccupation. Arturo Paoli writes, "If we are locked up in ourselves, blocked off to the point where our self is the center, we can free ourselves only by discovering the other and the others."[10] He is referring here firstly to God, the supreme "Other," and then to the other persons who surround us. It is to such a transcendence of our self-centeredness that Jesus calls us, according to Paoli:

> From what does Christ save us; what is salvation, redemption, liberation? . . . Christ rescued us from this loneliness, this being locked up, frozen in the self, and gave us the ability to discover and to communicate with the Other. This is the one thing that we are radically and incurably unable to do by ourselves.[11]

Christ is, for Christians, the reaching out of that mighty Other who is God; he is therefore the focus through which we respond in love. That much is understandable, but surely love of God with our entire being precludes our paying much attention to the world?

Since God both creates and loves the world, our love for God must also embrace the creation itself. But that means recognizing ourselves as units within a complexity that is so vast and hazardous that we would rather shrink from it, etherealize it, or cut it down to size than take it seriously enough to love it.

The ancient Stoics faced the uncertainties of the world by putting it firmly in its place. Since there are many things and persons whom we cannot control or securely possess, and since they are therefore the potential sources of anger, sorrow, loss, and frustration, let us be detached from them, let us find peace in splendid self-containment.

More subtle than the Stoics, many Idealists have avoided painful engagement with the world by reducing everything to the status of idea. They can then invent a religion of tranquility that, by calming the tempest of our reactions, achieves a "still point" in which ideas are at rest.

Interesting because, in some of its shapes, more modern and "scientific," is the tendency to lose the sharp pain of our involvement with the world by denying all personal responsibility. My sympathetic and parasympathetic nervous systems are to account for all dimensions of my failure to handle things. All is made satisfactory by Valium.

In a sense, all these devices are ways of turning inward, of locating our problem outside whatever we are responsible for and wherever we "find" ourselves to be. Christians may often be very uncomfortable to find themselves thrust into an enigmatic world by an enigmatic Creator, but they have repudiated repudiation of the world. They may very well find moments of relief in some exercise of withdrawal, but they cannot rest with subjectivism. It is a useful symbol that one of the best-known sentences in the New Testament admits of two equally possible translations: either "the Kingdom of God is within you," or "the Kingdom of God is in the midst of you" (Luke 17:21). For Christians it is and must be both, and it cannot be within until they have found it between themselves and the others who surround them.

So the Christian's fundamental experience is not contentless consciousness or boundlessness, but love. Assured of being loved by God, he or she is drawn into a net of love for others. Yet there *is* most assuredly within the Bible a repudiation of something that is sometimes called "the world," so we must ask what this means.

Thomas Merton has answered this question as succinctly as anyone. The "world" which is to be denied is

> the unquiet city of those who live for themselves and are therefore divided against one another in a struggle that cannot end. . . . It is the city of those who are fighting for possession of limited things and for the monopoly of goods and pleasures that cannot be shared by all.[12]

This means that we are to avoid the "world" of selfishness and exclusiveness, but not the actual world of persons and things who are in need of our love. Merton criticizes those who think of contemplation or meditation as a withdrawal from the sometimes painful struggle for reunion with others and says to them, "You do not know what contemplation is and you will never find God in your contemplation. For it is precisely in the recovery of our union with our brothers in Christ that we discover God and know Him."[13]

So we are not to become detached from our neighbors, but truly to find them and to find God in them. With this I agree, but there are some who have been so deeply wounded by the world that this is a difficult command; for them another way may be available, a way whose end is not other than Merton and Buber have described, but whose approach is different.

One of the most disturbing of fairly modern thinkers was Søren Kierkegaard, whose journey from despair to hope, from anguish to joy has been fragmentarily described in his books. In one of them he makes a fascinating distinction between two men, one of whom we can recognize as a rather typical, if old-fashioned, "religious" enthusiast and the other of whom he presents as a masculine example of the authentic Christian.[14]

The first is called the "knight of infinite resignation," and like the Stoic he has repudiated everything in order to become free, untroubled, and safe. He is serene and dignified—and vastly admired. But the other, the "knight of faith," is quite different. He enjoys his pipe, his food, his friends, and whatever he owns. What may puzzle us about him, however, is that while he looks very like the ordinary worldling, he is different in one respect. He is not shattered when he loses something he has enjoyed, or fails to obtain something he desires. He may stroll home after work, celebrating to a friend the exquisite meal his wife has probably prepared for him, but if, when he sees her, she laments a difficult day and offers him hot dogs, he is not in the least upset. On the contrary, hot dogs are wonderful!

What makes the knight of faith so strange? It is that he has once made the movement of infinite resignation, giving up his possessiveness entirely. He has renounced the whole world for God's sake, stripping himself of all claims, all hopes in order to stand clear of every rival interest and discover God. But then, because God is who and what he is, our knight has found himself receiving the whole world back again as God's gift! So he laughs with a truly liberated laughter and henceforth is possessed by none of his possessions but is free to enjoy what may be enjoyed and to do without what he may not have. Having even turned aside from persons, with their propensity for hurting and healing, he can now turn to them again unafraid.

I have long been torn between the Buberian image of finding God only in and through the world and the Kierkegaardian one of being set free to enjoy the world through finding God. I think both images are faithful to different personalities and that divine grace is able to enrich either of these ways of coming to God. What is perhaps most significant is that for both these methods the world is not lost when God is found, but it actually becomes dearer to us, although shorn of its power to drive us to despair.

Loving God and loving the world are, then, intimately related experiences—so intimately that it is hard to separate them. But what do we mean by "love"?

There are many things called by the single word "love." For many people it means a spontaneous feeling of attraction. This feeling cannot be commanded, and when it goes, the love is simply over. Marriages based on this sort of love are doomed to brevity, or to linger in a miserable afterglow, unless in the course of them another sort of love is found.

For others, love is the name of the sense of non-difference, of fusion and oneness in which we feel ourselves melt into the same Absolute that absorbs everyone else. This is a love that must lose its object and become, therefore, itself obsolete at last, for an Absolute has nothing to love.

For the Christian, "love" is what the New Testament means by its Greek word "agape." This is not a feeling, although it breeds feelings, and it takes careful note of the integrity and otherness of whatever is loved. It is the active seeking to serve the other. It is unpossessive, unmanipulative, but decidedly *not* uninvolved. The person who loves another in this way does not stand "above" him or her in detached benevolence, but stands beside him or her in the recognition that each may contribute something to the maturing wholeness of the other.

To love God means no less than to participate by our service in God's eternal becoming, and to love our human neighbor is to support him or her in whatever way we can.

Perhaps it should be noted that the command to "love your neighbor" does not mean that we must somehow be constantly busy trying to meet the need of everyone in the world; such a command would be absurd. The focus of this command is made clear by the parable of the Good Samaritan which is a response to the question "Who is my neighbor?" It is clear that the neighbor is not everyone, but at any given moment the number of my neighbors is limited to those upon whom my life can have some beneficent effect.

One of the things that may be unique about Christianity, then, is its emphasis on a kind of love that is a deliberate, concerned attention to the other in his or her singularity and particular need. I do not mean that other religions lack a teaching about the importance of loving, but I mean that where many great traditions, especially those centered upon altered states of consciousness, regard God or the Buddha Nature or Brahman or Nirvana as in essence some form of consciousness or of supraconsciousness, Christianity clings stubbornly to the precarious vision that "God is love" (1 John 4:8). God *is* love. This does not mean that love is God—that is, that anything we experience as love is the ultimate value—but that God, the Creator and Creative Ground of whose self-expression all that exists is a part, is more completely, more deeply, more wholly love than anything else. Of course, the love that God is is the sun of which anything we can mean by the word is merely the shadow, but it is of the utmost importance that for the Christian it is acceptable to say that God is love, and not at all acceptable to say "God is Consciousness" or "God is Mind-Only" or anything of the sort.

Love is, then, not merely a means to an end beyond itself, but the beginning of our being what we are meant to be. And, as we have seen, the love to which we refer is a sensitive appreciation of others and their need, given actual expression in our living toward the meeting of that need.

From the biblical perspective, much that passes for even self-sacrificial love is really not the love that brings us close to God. Saint Paul writes, "If I give away all I have, and if I deliver my body to be burned, but have not love, I gain nothing" (1 Cor. 13:3). So there can be an ultimate self-sacrifice that is not love! We can be willing to be burned "for the good of others" and yet not *love* them! What an alarming thought that is. But it penetrates to the heart of our generosity by showing that this is all too often disguised self-admiration. The truth is that we can serve others in such a way, or from such a motive, that they are not "ends" but means to our own concern for self-perfection. Our self-sacrifice can be the ultimate self-gratification. We must actually forget about perfecting ourselves and simply give ourselves to God and our neighbor *for their sake entirely.* The difficulty of doing this with a perfectly unambivalent spirit makes it necessary that God lend us aid; that aid is in part what Christian theology recognizes in Christian experience as the Holy Spirit.

The love that is central to Christianity does not dissolve the reality of one's own personhood, of God's otherness, or of the reality of other persons and things. Indeed, love is the discovery of the seriousness of these things and the learning to value them. A love that brings us into non-discriminating "unity" with All is by no means the same thing. As Paoli has written, "To annul the Other, religiosity is a more radical course than atheism. . . . It closes the door through which the Other might be able to enter by surprise."[15]

Here is another area in which Christianity refuses to be identified with the exaltation of subjectivity. God is the supreme *Relator,* and our proper response through which our being is fulfilled is, then, to relate to God and to each other, to turn *outward* toward the other, not inward to the deep self. Turning inward can, at best, gather our forces for the movement out to the world and its Creator; if it becomes itself the end of our efforts, we are short-circuited and our most "spiritual" attainments are no more than beautiful abortions.

Maternal and Paternal Religion

There are many convenient, but imperfect, ways of classifying religious traditions. One that seems to have a little pertinence in our discussion at this point is the distinguishing of "maternal" and "paternal" types of spirituality.

Maternal spirituality is grounded in the idea that our emergence from the womb of Reality is a kind of misfortune. When it makes the additional assumption that what is "real" must be good, the conclusion is reached that our individuality, being a misfortune, must also be less than real, perhaps a kind of illusion. In any case, our wholeness consists in our returning to that prenatal condition in which there is neither self nor other, in which awareness is clean of distinctions and we have been reabsorbed into Being, our eternal Mother. But this is to refuse to take seriously our birth and to ask what obligation it laid upon us.

Paternal spirituality, on the other hand, stresses our separation from the Divine, who is conceived as our Father. Our individuality is now real and our grave danger is alienation, the loss of all relationship with God. Such religion is often harsh, unforgiving, and unrelenting. Such a God is the supreme Judge, and our connection with this God tends to be legalistic: we must obey all the rules or be disinherited. As maternalistic religion can produce a tranquil rejection or at least minimizing of otherness, paternalistic religion can lead to a kind of submission that diminishes us.

Maternal religion, thus, stresses the imminence of the divine in us, tends to be pantheistic or monistic, and reaches its fulfillment in the unitive consciousness. Paternal religion stresses the transcendence and irreducible otherness of God, tends toward monotheism, and finds fulfillment in some form of relatedness, often with a heavy stress on law.

Christianity has often fallen toward the paternalistic side of religion, although some of its mystics have clearly leaned to the other. What too often escapes notice is that it is rooted in a perspective that is neither paternalist nor maternalist but stands above both in a way that is difficult to express.

The God of Christian perspective is not really Father or Mother, although both metaphors can be used. God is, rather, Inclusive Otherness, in whom we have our beings but in whom we genuinely have *our* beings.

One way of trying to assert this view and establish the ground for this experience is to present God as coming among us in the person of a male enfleshment of Christness, but one which is born from a virgin woman and in whose birth, therefore, no male has a role. This doctrine of the virgin birth of Jesus has always provided a difficulty for many Christians, since it violates our regular experience. Among liberals, the inclination has often been to abandon it altogether. After all, the New Testament can hardly be said to be full of the idea. Paul makes no reference to it; neither does Mark or John. Matthew gives it only the barest of ambiguous attention, and it is chiefly to Luke that we owe whatever we know about it. Surely, it is argued, so strange an event, and so important if true, would have been more central to the thinking of the early Christians than this scant attention indicates.

The virgin birth of him in whom we find the Christ, whatever difficulties it presents for us, is at the very least a remarkable way of stating that neither maleness nor femaleness is of advantage in the sight of God, and this God's relating to us is neither simply maternal nor paternal. God neither absorbs us into an undifferentiated Self nor casts us out into absolute separation. God is, as we have said, Inclusive Otherness—a term that violates logic but expresses a perception that is born within the Christian perspective.

One consequence of this is that God is not the *whole* truth about *us*, all that is left when illusion is abandoned. Another is that God is not to be encountered simply at our whim or produced through some manipulation of our consciousness. God is free of us (in this, paternalistic religion is correct) and cannot be commanded. No discipline, meditative or other, can infallibly bring the divine Presence to our consciousness, and whatever can be produced by our actions is not God. On the other hand (and here maternalistic religion comes closer to the truth), by deliberate intention God does come, and it is therefore true that if we ask we shall receive, if we seek we shall find, if we knock the door will be opened (Luke 11:9–10). But the asking, seeking, and knocking must be wholehearted, and we must be prepared to let God be God and not some projection of our subjectivity. We must even be prepared to *wait* for God.

The Christian's God may well be said to judge, but that judgment exists within God's love; without such judgment—the undeceived recognition of what we are—there can be no real love, but only infatuation or a tolerance that is really a version of indifference.

Once again, then, we see that the Christian must reject the unitive consciousness as a full understanding of God.

God's Action and Ours

Simply stated, it is not our *experience* that "saves" or fulfills us, but God's action. Our patient acceptance of God's action in the Christ, calling us, loving us, forgiving us, transforms radically our understanding and evaluation of all our experiences. This is not a difficult idea, but one so fundamental that it merits reiteration.

We are always inclined to judge whether we are "whole" by how we feel or by what satisfying state of subjectivity we have achieved. Against this the New Testament declares unyieldingly that however we feel and whatever our state of mind, our salvation, our movement toward perfection and wholeness, is rooted in God's acceptance of us, and this is not to be reduced to some condition we can manipulate within ourselves. Our acceptance of God's acceptance liberates us from self-centered concern about our own holiness or spiritual attainment, and directs us outward in self-forgetful service in and for the world about us.

The experience of "dropping the ego," as stated earlier, is at least closely akin to part of the Christian's adventure; but it must be emphasized that this is not a deliberate achievement so much as a gift received, something that is being done for us. To stand in simple openness with wonder and awe before the God who offers us the Christ is to recognize that what was thought of as our "self" was an unsatisfactory construction. It was only a collection of hopes, fears, tastes, prejudices, reluctances, adopted values, and so on. It is as if we had been a pastiche of borrowed pieces and colors. Gently, and ever so kindly, we find the Christ-presence disclosing to us the falsity of these accretions. Certainly, not all of them are without value, but the sum of them is not all we should have been and none of them is our inner integrity. We find ourselves learning the courage to see not only the first glimpse we may ever have had of the true self that lies beneath the motley garments, but also the sometimes bizarre nature of the garments themselves. Although it is not always easy to take them off, in the end there is nothing else to do.

Finally we discover that our whole life has been devoted to trying to *be* something—hence the accumulation of qualities and characteristics we thought we were. We have been trying to "make a name" for ourselves (as the Tower of Babel story puts it) when all that was asked was that we accept a name. Our belonging to the christing God *is* our name, and in that name, that reality, we can now begin to move and to build a new personhood, something of a work of personal art that is our response to God's love. Alas, we spend so long without our true name, so long trying to forge an identity out of the admiration of others or ourself, out of the satisfaction of impulse or the cultivation of "spirituality": God has named us, has given us our authenticity as a becoming-person, and we can shape nothing adequate until we have first accepted that.

Swami Chinmayananda has said,

> The final peak of success aimed at by a mind in meditation is its own merger into the great "silence"—into the dynamic Pure Consciousness which is the "matrix" behind all the subtle world of subjective thoughts-and-emotions, and the gross realm of objective things-and-beings.[16]

How different is the Christian gospel as Paul presents it:

> For by grace you have been saved through faith; and this is not your own doing, it is the gift of God—not because of works, lest any man should boast. For we are his workmanship, created in Christ Jesus for good works, which God prepared beforehand, that we should walk in them. (Eph. 2:8–10)

This Christian goal is no merging into a silence, but the acceptance of a transforming gift that directs us to action. What it demands of us is firstly trust in God. But how simple is trusting? Is it not one of the hardest things for us to do? All our inclinations lead us to want to *achieve.* Our culture (and almost every other) conditions us by subtly suggesting that the race goes to the swift; the ideals of rugged individualism and the infamous Protestant Work Ethic combine to make us suspicious of anything we may have freely. Above all, our pride makes us wish to be fully responsible for what we become. Thus the news that our fulfillment is God's gift is "good news" only after we have accepted the bad news that the best we can do is not enough; we do not reach God—God reaches us. It is only *then* that our work of self-creating becomes sufficient. Until we have realized and accepted this fact, our highest attainment, even our greatest mystical achievement, is a vacuous pomposity.

If the Christian's good news is welcomed by us, however, it is good news indeed, and for whatever sort of person we are. For romanticists, the gospel indicates that the Spirit of God may dwell within us, and that is news they like to hear. But they must also hear a criticism of all religiosity, all mystical or spiritual programs that aim at the development of our own souls, for the gospel says that God is not to be manipulated, but is that Spirit for whom we must be prepared to wait.

For the intellectual, the gospel comes with the good/bad news that while our intellects are limited and cannot think all the thoughts of God, yet there is a *logos* in the universe, a light that enlightens us all, and this finds its most important brightness in the Christ, the "*logos* made flesh."

For the realist, the gospel makes it clear that matter and energy are creatures of God which participate in divine Being; they are not base cosmic catastrophes. They may rise to the quality we call "spirit" without losing their nature as matter and energy. Indeed, so compatible are the spheres of matter and spirit that the Christ is the materiality of the divine Spirit. Yet there is bad news with this, too. "Flesh and blood," we are told, "cannot inherit the kingdom of God" (1 Cor. 15:50). Preoccupation with the purely material or worldly for its sake alone, "materialism" in its various forms, is shallow, unfulfilling, and misleading.

Finally, the good news of God's persistent invitation to us is addressed, with its corresponding bad news, to all our potencies of consciousness. If it is true that the "logical" West chiefly uses the left hemisphere of the brain and is therefore excessively analytical and verbal, while the "mysterious" East develops the right hemisphere and is therefore holistic in its viewing, non-logical (as regards its highest perceptions), and non-verbal, Christianity dismisses (but not unkindly) attempts to make either of these a "higher" way of experiencing. Its sobering message is that we need to be healed; we need "salvation" in respect of both halves of our brain!

We are inclined to be separated from God in both our reason and our intuition, and it is as whole persons that we need to be gathered into the creative continuum that is God's life. We need grace—

and the tricky thing is that grace is not an "experience" we can have. We can experience joy in our confidence that grace has been given; we can experience our readiness to be given that grace; we can experience a sense of the divine nearness, the diminishment of self-concern, and so on. But grace is the name for God's action. It embraces us, even if we are unaware of it. In my mood of blackest despair, when my biorhythms are at their lowest and my students at their worst, God's grace is as effective as ever—and *that* is a fact more important than my mood. We are invited to trust in that grace, and to that end it has been visible variously in history, to whoever has eyes to see, but visible preeminently as the Christ.

What does all this mean for meditation and its modifications of consciousness? It means that these may indeed be useful; they may well offer us important promises of new forms of psychotherapy, an enrichment of our sensitivity to many things, and a new appreciation of intuition. All this is good, even very good; but from the Christian perspective more is needed. Without the simple-hearted response to God's christing, that "more" will never be ours.

Those who seek to make themselves strong in spirit by some kind of meditative exercise are, after all, rather like those who try to make themselves strong in body by rigorous muscle-building: "I was an eighty-pound weakling until . . ." is not so different from "I was an anxiety-ridden and shallow soul until I tried Guru So-and-so's meditation method." Spiritual muscles acquired by our own efforts are not much more valuable than physical ones, and are even a little more dangerous; the more of them we have, the less we are likely to recognize our own relativity, our finitude, the necessity and inescapable ambiguity of our perceptions. At last we may actually identify completely with the cosmos or with Cosmic Spirit or Mind, utterly forgetting the continuing transience and gross limitation of ourselves as instruments for awareness.

Indeed, one may wonder whether one of the benefits of meditation may not be counterproductive in some ways. Anxiety, uncomfortable tension, confusion in the face of a complex world—these are certainly not experiences we enjoy. But tension and even anxiety are not always or necessarily bad. A certain amount of discomfort is needed for most forms of creativity. It simply is not true that a perfectly calm, satisfied, tranquil mind is inventive. A contented Columbus does not discover America; a thoroughly peaceful mortal does not discover God—and probably does not even invent the safety pin.

The Christian whose faith is strong does, indeed, enjoy a kind of peace, but it is of a strange sort, for it contains within it enough tension in the Christian's relations with the world to drive him or her to continuing creative and healing concern.

No Self or New Self

Many religious systems regard the "self" of the human being as a worthless set of acquired attitudes. If we could only get rid of all this junk, removing the false self-images, dropping the encrusting values and concepts, we would be clean of limitation, of self—we would be pure and perfect. We would have, then, no fear, because fear arises out of our false belief in a false identity, a spurious individuality and selfhood.

One must ask, in what sense is the self false? Certainly it is an accumulation of learned responses, acquired traits and other things, but why false? Is it false in the sense that it really is not "there" at all? Obviously not, or we would not be urged to get rid of it. Is it false in the sense that a painting of surpassing beauty is also false? The painted landscape is not really "there" but is an invention of the artist. It is painted onto the "reality" of a canvas. If this is the sense in which the self is false—as a work which this particular human organism has created—it may still be a work of art, and it may still have splendor and value.

If they are true to their biblical background, Christians do not believe that they have any inherently immortal self. Rather, they believe that they are at the center of a potentiality given its reality by God. As such they are organisms engaged in becoming something, becoming *persons* and, if they should learn to fulfill themselves through relation to God and the world, becoming spiritual persons.

The continuation of what the Christian constructs is dependent on grace—on God's act of treasuring what has worth—and since the Christian regards individuality as itself part of a person's potential, he or she assumes that even this is capable of being treasured. Meanwhile, day by day, decision by decision, experience by experience, the Christian becomes something, and because loyalty to God is the central fact of this becoming, there is a coherence about the Christian's life, an essential shape to his or her emerging personhood.

But the material for the construction of a Christian self is not found in a mere self-emptying. This shedding of things does continuously occur, for we grow beyond old ideas and values, but it is not the primary business of our life. The building of our personhood derives its material chiefly from our encounter with God and with the world, through our daily experience, and it is sound material when our encounters are themselves shaped by our supreme loyalty to that God whose exciting embrace of the entire creation is illuminated for us by divine christing Presence in the life of Jesus.

The Christian does not find that he or she is becoming a no-self, but a *new* self, fully individual, always limited, but part of the mysterious creativity of God. Commitment in self-dedicating love, rather than introspection or simple detachment, can bring about this exhilarating consequence.

Consciousness and Idolatry

There is a final theological comment that must be approached very gently. Certainly, most of those who are ardently involved in recommending altered consciousness are not deliberately seducing their clientele. Nevertheless, for all too many persons the achievement in consciousness of meditational disciplines may be said to be a form of idolatry.

When our God, our spiritual focus, is something we can precipitate, something contained within ourselves, it is an idol. Dominique Barthélemy says that idolatry is the name of that act whereby humans "replace the unbearable presence of the utterly free and all powerful being with another, product of his skill and dreams, instantly tamed because it is born of his own subjectivity."[17]

Our wanting to *be* god, to avoid awe, to be entirely self-constructive, instead of submitting to the influence of the divine Other, can lead us to idolize a state of awareness. To paraphrase Barthélemy, instead of allowing God to shape us by breaking in us whatever is false, we prefer to avoid the pain of that experience by shaping God to our liking out of the materials of our own consciousness.[18]

Over and over again the Bible insists that the "fear" of God— that is, the awe we must feel in the presence of that overwhelming One whose majesty is unimaginable—is the beginning of wisdom. The arrogance of the fundamentalist Christian who reduces God (or at least God's options for action) to the words of a book, the sentimentality of the liberal who makes God our sibling, and the idolatry of the unitive mystic who identifies his or her own "highest" state of consciousness with God are alike tragic falsifications. They are rebuked by the quite different kind of experience that the Bible presents to us as encounter with God. Consider the book of Exodus where God is thunderous at Sinai; the book of Job where God is enigmatic, uncontrollable, but strangely satisfying; Isaiah's sixth chapter where God makes the prophet aware of human frailty and personal unworthiness before the shaken and awestruck man is healed and given work to do. The experience of Peter before the Christ ("Depart from me, for I am a sinful man, O Lord" [Luke 5:9]) or of Paul, or of the assembled disciples in the famous upper room—all these bespeak the experience not of a "great silence" but of the dramatic coming of One who is unalterably other than ourselves, yet in whose being we exist.

Through consciousness, we do experience God; but from the Christian perspective, God is not our consciousness, nor is God ever reducible to *any* state of it.

One Conclusion

Jacques Ellul has said that the Christian is called to *be* something even more than he or she is called to achieve something. We are not primarily or exclusively invited to struggle to *achieve* righteousness; God *calls* us righteous and we must accept that naming of us. We need not work at the hard task of being lovable: God loves us! We relax, therefore, in divine love and find within ourselves a growing capacity for loving without self-interest. When we accept God's naming of us— which is to accept God—we begin to plan not so much to build things as to *be* something new. We do not construct a ready-made system of justice; *we are just.* We do not exhaust ourselves trying to force an un-

yielding society to be righteous; *we are righteous*. And we do not somehow bring peace wholesale by some clever manipulation upon the
earth; *we are peaceful.*[19]

Ellul is reminding us here of something easily forgotten. He is
not decrying action—indeed, he wants Christians to become true revolutionaries—but he is saying that Christian action flows from Christian
personhood, and that this is a gift received progressively from God. But
this gift, this hallowing presence of God, will not truly be found by introversion. God meets us in all the persons and things of our daily lives
when we learn to wait quietly there. God is sublimely, disturbingly,
and instructively present in the Christ, whom we may come to know if
we walk with him through the pages of the New Testament and try to
see behind his words to the Presence that inspired them. Meditation
may prepare our sensitivity, but it cannot produce God as if God were a
rabbit in a hat and meditation the supreme magician.

As Thomas Merton has it,

> To say that I am made in the image of God is to say that love is the
> reason for my existence, for God is love. . . . And so one of the worst
> illusions in the life of contemplation would be to try to find God by
> barricading yourself inside your own soul, shutting out all external real-
> ity by sheer concentration and will-power.[20]

Another Conclusion

It may seem that, in trying to represent a Christian perspective,
we have been arguing for the superiority of Christianity as a religious
tradition. It is important here to say that this has not been the intention. No Christian is obliged to believe that his or her religion knows
all the truth there is, or that it has not perpetrated, through ardent advocates, horrors against humanity. We have only one major point to
make: God, for the Christian, is active *everywhere*, and when anyone
encounters God it is not primarily because of any doctrine, any meditative or other practice, any ritual. We meet God because God is a
christing One who comes to us and rewards our readiness with grace,
and it would be absurdly arrogant for Christians to assume that God is
not active through traditions other than their own.

Properly understood, the Christ is the act of God for all of us, and Christianity, as a tradition, has no monopoly on the Divine. Someone who does not recognize in Jesus the concrete expression, once for all, of that divine grace may well be, nevertheless, its recipient; and someone who acknowledges the *dogma* that Jesus is the Christ may miss the grace because he or she makes a god of the dogma.

In short, Christianity is not the Christ, and it may even become demonic when it fails to be simply the bearer of the good news that this world has seen the presence of that unique "concrete universal" through which God is constantly inviting us all to renewed relationship.

8

Tentative Evaluations

It is a very common human experience to feel incomplete, not quite "whole" or not yet "there." We may not know what or where "there" is, but we have an impulse to find it, and religion may usually be understood as one of the attempts to do so. In fact, one might say that virtually any enterprise aiming at really fulfilling or satisfying oneself is an attempt to find the way to the "there" of our life. Some persons stress the attainment of a persuasive and coherent philosophy, others more simply the formulation of a supreme value or of a hierarchy of values. Romantics and mystics seek a satisfying experience of some other sort which they often characterize as cosmic consciousness, ecstasy, union with the Absolute, perfect tranquility, or, perhaps, an awareness that is holistic and beyond the more common consciousness of things.

Meditation has become one popular method of reaching the desired haven of wholeness, however this is defined or understood. It is important, therefore, realistically to appraise the values and the possible errors or dangers that are contained in theories and practices of meditation.

The valuable contributions that some forms of meditation may make to certain persons include at least the following:

(1) The retreat into inwardness can sometimes help us to return to the world with a refreshed way of seeing things. Colors may seem more vivid or subtle, shapes appear with a clarity they had lost for us through our habituation to them, and there is a wonderful "realness"

about things. Since one of the roots of boredom is the losing of the capacity to sense objects with such appreciative openness, and since our customary world-view grows stale and needs to be opened by a new receptivity, some meditative experiences seem able to instill a renewal of interest in and even delight in the universe about us. Whether or not this is achieved because we have a "bimodal consciousness" or a "split brain" is not important here. The rest from stressful or habituated patterns of thought and perception seems often to lead to a less selective and blasé attention to our environment and a new enjoyment of it.

(2) Relaxation and calmness appear to be frequent products of some fairly simple meditation techniques. The drawing in of our attention and the slowing or temporary stilling of the flow of thought, sensation, and emotion may provide for some a useful means of recovering poise and self-possession.

(3) The centering of our attention may, as Martin Buber has suggested, gather our forces, so to speak, and enable us to launch out into engagement with the world more wholeheartedly, more *totally*, than we could before. This means that we may act more perceptively, relate to other persons more deeply, and offer ourselves more efficiently to whatever needs us.

(4) If the intuitive or holistic grasp of meanings, patterns, or other realities and what Polanyi means by "tacit understanding" really are produced or released by meditation, a form of sensitivity and apprehension that operates only restrictedly in the usual flow of linear and logical thought may be another benefit of meditation.

Further, if meditation can enable us to collect our scattered attention and focus it on a *Gestalt*, a "whole," rather than on a multitude of parts and aspects, then, as Polanyi says, we may "see" meanings, functions, and values of that "whole" which had eluded us before. To grasp a "philosophy of life" in this way would, for example, mean to understand it more completely and to enter into it with our entire commitment. Let it be noted, however, that such commitment is by no means free of danger, because even focal and holistic attention may not guarantee the truth or adequacy of what we thus see. Roberto Assagioli, among many others, has indicated the need for the critical expertise of linear thought to be applied to what holistic or intuitive experience accepts uncritically.

(5) It has sometimes been argued that meditation can produce an enhancement of creativity. Where someone has been immobilizd by a weight of tension and anxiety beyond his or her capacity to handle, this claim may well prove accurate. However, it is also asserted that *some* tension is quite necessary for creativity, and this means that if meditation produces a too thorough equanimity it may actually destroy our power to think either critically or innovatively. More data is needed here, but it seems to me that the art of an extremely intuitive procedure such as Zen shows a strong tendency to become, after a while, repetitive and stagnant. My own informal and very unscientific observation of Zen students suggests that there often is a temporary improvement in the ability to deal creatively with ideas, but that this is often nullified in a depressing blandness after a time—while the subject continues to believe he or she is performing well.

Let us say, then, that the appropriate modification of excessive tension can be useful, but the achievement of the right degree of tension may require a critical and analytical ability rather than a holistic or meditative one.

(6) It has long been claimed that some of the more exotic forms of meditation produce extraordinary physiological effects. Yogins are occasionally said to be able, for example, to reduce their rate of breathing and their flow of blood to near immobility. Shamans are said to walk on fire without being burned, to pierce their flesh with pins or knives without pain or bleeding; some have even claimed to be enabled by their discipline to levitate.

One may be skeptical about some of these accomplishments, but those that are real may promise quite tangible benefits. To be able to suspend leakage of blood from a wound, to decelerate the heart at will—such achievements could be useful therapeutic procedures. Indeed, it is already clear that some things claimed for yogins can be accomplished by the most ordinary of us by such unmystical methods as biofeedback.

(7) The experience of "dropping" old identifications following the "blink" of awareness to which we have frequently referred, may well be significant psycho-therapeutically for persons who are caught in untenable and unrealistic assumptions and unproductive self-understandings. There are dangers in this experience, but properly

controlled it may well have considerable value as a means toward clearing away inept identifications and thus facilitating new and more efficient ones.

These, then, are some possible advantages to be gained from meditation and its altered states of awareness. What potential hazards are presented to us by the popularity of meditation, and what reservations must we maintain?

(1) An overvaluing of unitive, holistic consciousness may easily lead us to distrust or devalue too much our use of analytical and practical reason. This may be serious socially as well as individually, and it is to be observed that societies in which non-discriminating or unitive awareness is highly prized tend to be weak not only in science but also in social reform and the amelioration of gross and ancient inequities. Whatever may be said in partial defense of it, the long survival in India of a rigid caste system which expressed, among other things, racial antipathy is an example of what I mean.

(2) Meditation that pushes us very deeply into ourselves may be extremely dangerous if we have not been properly prepared for the experience. For instance, the "blink" and loss of ego-identification enable us to survive what may otherwise be simply a profound psychological trauma. Failing such preparation, the result may be an irreversible psycho-pathological withdrawal. Mass indulgence in popular meditation techniques may, therefore, be irresponsible and may even reflect, in those who promote them, a cynical disregard (interpreted as unattached benevolence) for the integrity and particularity of individuals.

(3) Freud, Alexander, and others have pointed to regression and even narcissism as perhaps the most objectionable features of meditation, and some observers seem to see a lamentable tendency to a subtle selfishness in many practicers today. Non-attached compassion—an oft-promised result of meditation—sometimes turns out to be an exploitation of others for our own "spiritual" ends.

(4) Regression to a more primitive and uncritical form of thought is the danger that Leuba and others see in these states of consciousness. It may even be that our evolution as a species is prejudiced by the current tendency to reject the struggle to refine laboriously our logical and analytical reason, and by the easy acceptance of synthetic or

holistic perceiving. This may not be a very imminent danger, but it may increase to the extent that mystical or similar forms of awareness are valued by many as "higher" rather than simply different mental functions.

(5) In a time when the precise command of language seems already to be rare, one may worry that facility for communication may be further diminished as definition, analysis, and verbal skills of all sorts are rated less important than the enjoyment of ineffable—that is, non-verbal and inexpressible—experiences.

(6) Theological warnings about the danger of mistaking *any* form of consciousness (or emotion) for God are worthy of consideration. A God (that is, our focus of highest allegiance, that which we consider worthy of our supreme commitment) who does not draw us *out* of ourselves in service to the world becomes merely the final stamp of approval on our narcissism.

It may be useful to reiterate, in this connection, the relation between prayer and meditation. Prayer, when it is not just a mumbling of words, may concentrate our attention as surely as any system of meditation, but since it is a reaching out, a looking with all our heart, mind, and spirit *beyond* ourselves—in short, an intense *relating*—it should escape the danger of excessive introjection. Some Christians have found, it is true, that certain of the popular methods of meditation can be adapted to improve their experience of prayer, and there are even some fairly interesting "How to Do It" books on the subject, such as Robert F. Willett's *Primer for Christian Meditation*. But in these cases, it is the subject's experience of prayer, not necessarily the act of relating with God, that is enhanced.

Conclusion

Much of the data presented so far in studies of meditation may be questioned, and this applies even to that gathered in recent investigations of physiological concomitants of changes in consciousness. Interpretations of this data are even more vulnerable to questioning, and it would be a grave mistake to assume that some puissant discipline such as "Modern Psychology" has established beyond doubt the values or disvalues of any of the procedures we have discussed.

But meditation is a fact, and the experiences it engenders seem worthy of serious investigation. Whether our interest is spurred by secular or religious impulse, this is a time for caution and for avoiding extravagant assumptions. Some benefits are surely to be derived from meditation by some persons, but more harm than good is likely to follow if it is assumed that *everyone* has something to gain from meditation, or if the often extreme claims (either religious or therapeutic) are accepted uncritically.

Epilogue

A Fantasy

It was two a.m., and all, at last, was quiet in the hospital. In the maternity ward activity was at a minimum. Almost all the mothers were sleeping, the last of the fathers had long since given up goggling at the product of his efforts, and the staff were drowsily going about their nocturnal routines.

Only in the nursery was there any intellectual activity, for there the newborn babies were thinking about the world they had entered. Already all of them had found that the world outside the womb was more hazardous than the dark security they had left, less reliable and more confusingly complex.

Was our coming a mistake? What shall we do with the puzzling and alarming universe we have stumbled into?

Some quickly determined to survive—at any cost. The world had many sharp edges, many rocky pathways. Well, then, we shall make use of even those features if we can, and if we must we will cushion them. With what? After the slightest pause the decision was made. We will make soft the sharp places and the needle points of danger with the bodies of those weaker and more pliable than ourselves. We will win a gentle place for ourselves by lining our nest with the soft flesh of the vulnerable. So these began to plan for living in the world, and they followed their paths with grim determination.

Others faced the future with fear and began to wonder how they might return to the safe obscurity of the womb. But it occurred to them that the womb was as impermanent as themselves, and with this realization, a deep horror began to spread through every channel of their brains. To turn back the creeping chill, these began to invent an invulnerable womb of the mind, and finding comfort in this, they also found it possible to survive. They talked together with soft smiles and without alarm, but they talked and would always talk as the unborn must do. They knew little rivalry and no great disturbances, but they also knew little of other things that life offered, for their adventures were only those that one can undertake in the womb. The roughness of the real world was hidden from them, but so were many of its rough splendors. Not knowing what they did not know, they came at last to think they had missed nothing.

There were others, too. Some found it a wonder to think that they had been thrust out of the womb into a world. It felt to them not like an end, but a beginning. What, then, could the end be? They could not guess, but they determined to find out. They would be faithful to whatever had called them from the gloom. They would cut themselves on the edges of the world, hurt themselves in a hundred ways, but they would be true to the demand thay they live and move in the world that awaited them.

Of these adventurers there were two kinds. Some really sought nothing but the journey itself, or were content to be on the road to something, without impatience to know what the end was like. Bravely they followed what seemed sometimes to be a path and sometimes to be no path, hoping for nothing very definite but intrigued by the traveling itself. They studied every stone, every ridge, tree, and mountain. They plunged into rivers and sought to know all they could about the sea. For many of them the learning they acquired was not a means to some end, but quite sufficient in itself.

Finally there were, of these explorers, a few who made a strange, elusive discovery. They found that they could sense, obscurely, in every inch of the way a Presence, as if of the mysterious Path-builder. They never knew so very much about him (or was it her?) but it seemed to them he or she lighted the way for them a little. A few were so delighted with this that they settled by the path in some place where the Presence had been strong and they built great temples there, proclaiming this to be the destiny and the journey over. There they lived their lives, settling down and never quite realizing that they were alone, for the Presence had moved on and their temples were empty except for themselves.

Others moved in obedience to the Presence without (which cast its shadow within them) and knew that every day they must decide once more whether to be faithful or not. They could not capture and enslave the "Thing" that moved ahead of them; they could not domesticate it. They could only follow, and even then they could not prove that they followed anything at all. Somehow they knew; there had been for all of them a glimpse of light. With this they had to be content and, strangely, this was enough and more than enough unless there overtook them the sickness of a pride that wanted not to be led so strangely but to possess something as predictable as a diamond in the hand.

Who was wise? Did they all reach what, and only what, they were faithful to? They each made for themselves a world through their own way of being alive, and to the end of the road most felt at home only in that world. But was any of these worlds closer to reality than the rest?

This is the hardest question of every world, for it is a question that must be answered in faith or not at all.

Notes

Chapter 1

1. Kilgore Trout, *Venus on the Half-Shell* (New York: Dell, 1974), 201.
2. Ibid.
3. Chintaharan Chakravarti, *Tantras: Studies on Their Religion and Literature* (Calcutta: Punthi Pustak, 1963), 38.
4. Cf. Lama Anagarika Govinda, *Foundations of Tibetan Mysticism* (New York: Dutton, 1960).

Chapter 2

1. Govinda, *Tibetan Mysticism*, 27.
2. John Blofeld, *The Jewel in the Lotus* (Westport, Conn.: Hyperion, 1948), 66–67.
3. Herbert V. Guenther, *The Tantric View of Life* (Berkeley and London: Shambala, 1972), 139.

Chapter 3

1. E. Kadloubovsky and G. E. H. Palmer, *Writings from the Philokalia, on Prayer of the Heart* (London: Faber and Faber, 1951).
2. A recent manual of Christian meditation makes interesting use of this ancient prayer. Cf. Robert F. Willett, *Primer for Christian Meditation* (Wilton, Conn.: Morehouse-Barlow, 1976).
3. Ignatius Loyola, *The Spiritual Exercises of St. Ignatius*, tr. Louis J. Puhl, S.J. (Maryland: Newman, 1951), 1.
4. Ibid., 112.
5. Saint Teresa, "The Life of the Holy Mother Teresa of Jesus," *The Complete Works of St. Teresa of Jesus*, tr. E. Allison Peers, (London: Sheed and Ward, 1946), 1:11.
6. Saint Teresa, "The Way of Perfection," *The Complete Works*, 2:17.
7. Ibid.
8. Ibid., 52.

9. Ibid., 93.
10. Ibid., 95.
11. Ibid., 104.
12. Ibid.
13. Ibid.
14. Ibid., 127.
15. Saint Teresa, "Conceptions of the Love of God," *The Complete Works*, 2:384.
16. Ibid.
17. Saint Teresa, "The Life of the Holy Mother Teresa of Jesus," *The Complete Works*, 1:105.
18. Ibid., 110.
19. Ibid., 112.
20. Ibid., 120.

Chapter 4

1. Sigmund Freud, *Civilization and Its Discontents*, tr. and ed. James Strachey (New York: Norton, 1961).
2. F. Alexander, "Buddhistic Training as an Artificial Catatonia," *Psychoanalytic Review* 18 (1931): 129–45.
3. James H. Leuba, *The Psychology of Religious Mysticism* (New York: Harcourt, Brace, 1925), 316.
4. Cf. Erich Fromm, *Psychoanalysis and Religion* (New Haven: Yale University, 1956), Chapter 2.
5. A compact summary of the research we have referred to in this section is contained in Victor F. Emerson, "Research on Meditation," *The R. M. Bucke Memorial Society Newsletter-Review* 5 (Spring 1972).
6. Ralph Ezios, "Implications of Physiological Feedback Training," *The Proper Study of Man*, ed. James Fadiman (New York: Macmillan, 1971), 465–76.
7. Claudio Naranjo and Robert E. Ornstein, *On the Psychology of Meditation* (New York: Viking, 1971), 167–68.
8. Arthur J. Deikman, "De-Automatization and the Mystic Experience," *Psychiatry* 29 (1966): 332.
9. Ibid., 333.
10. Ibid.
11. Marghanita Laski, *Ecstasy: A Study of Some Secular and Religious Experiences* (London: Cresset, 1961).
12. Deikman, "De-Automatization," 336.
13. Ibid., 337.
14. Arthur J. Deikman, "Bimodal Consciousness," *Archives of General Psychiatry* 25 (December 1971): 481–89. Reprinted in Robert E. Ornstein, ed., *The Nature of Human Consciousness* (San Francisco: Freeman, 1968), 68–86.

15. Ornstein, *Human Consciousness*, 68.
16. Cf. Joseph E. Bogen, "The Other Side of the Brain: An Appositional Mind," *Bulletin of the Los Angeles Neurological Societies* 34 (July 1969): 135ff.
17. Dorothy Lee, "Codifications of Reality: Lineal and Nonlineal" in *Freedom and Culture* (Englewood Cliffs, N.J.: Prentice-Hall, 1959), 113.
18. Ibid.
19. Roberto Assagioli, "Spiritual Psychosynthesis: Technique for the Use of Intuition" in *Psychosynthesis: A Manual of Principles and Techniques* (New York: Hobbs, Dorman, 1965), 219.
20. Michael Polanyi, *The Study of Man* (Chicago: University of Chicago, 1963).

Chapter 5

1. Norman Melchert, "Mystical Experience and Ontological Claims," *Philosophy and Phenomenological Research* 37 (June 1977): 445–63.
2. Ibid., 451.
3. Ibid., 452.
4. R. D. Laing, *The Divided Self* (Harmondsworth: Penguin, 1965), 44–45.
5. Melchert, "Mystical Experience," 455.
6. Ibid., 456.
7. John Blofeld, "Dharma: More Than Mere Ethics and Psychology," *The International Buddhist Forum Quarterly* Introductory Issue (1977): 6.
8. Michael Oakeshott, *Experience and Its Modes* (Cambridge: Cambridge University, 1933).
9. Ibid., 23.
10. Ibid., 25.
11. John Macmurray, *The Self as Agent*, vol. 1 of *The Form of the Personal* (New York: Harper and Brothers, 1957).
12. I have tried to develop a Process Theology more extensively in *Mystery and Meaning: Personal Logic and the Language of Religion* (Philadelphia: Westminster, 1975).
13. Govinda, *Tibetan Mysticism*, 23.
14. Ibid., 24.
15. Aśvaghosha, *The Awakening of Faith*, tr. Yoshito S. Hakeda (New York: Columbia University, 1967), 98.
16. Govinda, *Tibetan Mysticism*, 92.
17. Melchert, "Mystical Experience," 453.
18. Ibid., 454.
19. Ibid., 455.
20. William Kilpatrick, *Identity and Intimacy* (New York: Dell, 1975), 3.
21. Ibid.
22. Viktor E. Frankl, *Man's Search for Meaning* (New York: Washington Square, 1963).

23. Kilpatrick, *Identity and Intimacy*, *43.*
24. Ibid., 72.
25. Ibid., 74.
26. Peter L. Berger, *The Sacred Canopy* (Garden City, N.Y.: Doubleday, 1969), 56.

Chapter 7

1. William R. Uttal, *The Psychobiology of Mind* (Hillsdale, N.J.: Lawrence Erlbaum Associates, 1978), 5.
2. Ibid.
3. Cf. 1 Cor. 13:8–12.
4. Martin Buber, *I and Thou*, tr. Walter Kaufmann (New York: Scribner's, 1970), 134.
5. Ibid., 141.
6. Ibid., 128.
7. G. K. Chesterton, *The Secret of Father Brown* (New York: Penguin, 1975), 133.
8. Joseph Goldstein, *The Experience of Insight* (Santa Cruz: Unity, 1976) 2.
9. Naranjo and Ornstein, *Psychology of Meditation*, 79.
10. Arturo Paoli, *Meditations on Saint Luke*, tr. Bernard F. McWilliams (Maryknoll, N.Y.: Orbis, 1977), 48.
11. Ibid.
12. Thomas Merton, *New Seeds of Contemplation* (New York: New Directions Books, 1961), 78.
13. Ibid.
14. Cf. Søren A. Kierkegaard, *Fear and Trembling*, tr. Walter Lowrie (Princeton: Princeton University, 1968), 49ff.
15. Paoli, *Meditations on Saint Luke*, *74.*
16. Swami Chinmayananda, "Hasten Slowly," *What Is Meditation?* ed. John White (Garden City, N.Y.: Doubleday, 1974), 2–3.
17. Dominique Barthélemy, *Dieu et Son Image* (Paris: Les Editions du Cerf, 1973), 100–101. My translation.
18. Ibid.
19. Jacques Ellul, *The Presence of the Kingdom*, tr. Olive Wyon (New York: Seabury, 1967).
20. Merton, *New Seeds of Contemplation*, 60, 64.

Selected Bibliography

Literature cited

Alexander, F. "Buddhistic Training as an Artificial Catatonia." *Psychoanalytic Review* 18 (1931): 129–45.

Assagioli, Roberto. "Spiritual Psychosynthesis: Technique for the Use of Intuition." *Psychosynthesis: A Manual of Principles and Techniques.* New York: Hobbs, Dorman, 1965.

Aśvaghosha. *The Awakening of Faith.* Translated by Yoshito S. Hakeda. New York: Columbia University, 1967.

Barthélemy, Dominique. *Dieu et Son Image.* Paris: Les Editions du Cerf, 1973.

Berger, Peter L. *The Sacred Canopy.* Garden City, N.Y.: Doubleday, 1969.

Blofeld, John. "Dharma: More Than Mere Ethics and Psychology." *The International Buddhist Forum Quarterly* Introductory Issue (1977).

--------. *The Jewel in the Lotus.* Westport, Conn.: Hyperion, 1948.

Bogen, Joseph E. "The Other Side of the Brain: An Appositional Mind." *Bulletin of the Los Angeles Neurological Societies* 34 (July 1969).

Buber, Martin. *I and Thou.* Translated by Walter Kaufmann. New York: Scribner's, 1970.

Chakravarti, Chintaharan. *Tantras: Studies on Their Religion and Literature.* Calcutta: Punthi Pustak, 1963.

Chesterton, G. K. *The Secret of Father Brown.* New York: Penguin, 1975.

Deikman, Arthur J. "Bimodal Consciousness." *Archives of General Psychiatry* 25 (December 1971): 481–89.

--------. "De-Automatization and the Mystic Experience." *Psychiatry* 29 (1966): 324–38.

Ellul, Jacques. *The Presence of the Kingdom.* Translated by Olive Wyon. New York: Seabury, 1967.

Emerson, Victor F. "Research on Meditation." *The R. M. Bucke Memorial Society Newsletter-Review* 5 (Spring 1972).

Fadiman, James, ed. *The Proper Study of Man*. New York: Macmillan, 1971.

Fox, Douglas A. *Mystery and Meaning: Personal Logic and the Language of Religion*. Philadelphia: Westminster, 1975.

Frankl, Viktor E. *Man's Search for Meaning*. New York: Washington Square, 1963.

Freud, Sigmund. *Civilization and Its Discontents*. Translated and edited by James Strachey. New York: Norton, 1961.

Fromm, Erich. *Psychoanalysis and Religion*. New Haven: Yale University, 1956.

Goldstein, Joseph. *The Experience of Insight*. Santa Cruz: Unity, 1976.

Govinda, Lama Anagarika. *Foundations of Tibetan Mysticism*. New York: Dutton, 1960.

Guenther, Herbert V. *The Tantric View of Life*. Berkeley and London: Shambala, 1972.

Kadloubovsky, E., and G. E. H. Palmer. *Writings from the Philokalia, on Prayer of the Heart*. London: Faber and Faber, 1951.

Kierkegaard, Søren A. *Fear and Trembling*. Translated by Walter Lowrie. Princeton: Princeton University, 1968.

Kilpatrick, William. *Identity and Intimacy*. New York: Dell, 1975.

Laing, R. D. *The Divided Self*. Harmondsworth: Penguin, 1965.

Laski, Marghanita. *Ecstasy: A Study of Some Secular and Religious Experiences*. London: Cresset, 1961.

Lee, Dorothy. "Codifications of Reality: Lineal and Nonlineal." *Freedom and Culture*. Englewood Cliffs, N.J.: Prentice-Hall, 1959.

Leuba, James H. *The Psychology of Religious Mysticism*. New York: Harcourt, Brace, 1925.

Loyola, Ignatius. *The Spiritual Exercises of St. Ignatius*. Translated by Louis J. Puhl, S.J. Maryland: Newman, 1951.

Macmurray, John. *The Self as Agent*. New York: Harper and Brothers, 1957.

Melchert, Norman. "Mystical Experience and Ontological Claims." *Philosophy and Phenomenological Research* 37 (June 1977): 445–63.

Merton, Thomas. *New Seeds of Contemplation*. New York: New Directions, 1961.

Naranjo, Claudio, and Robert E. Ornstein. *On the Psychology of Meditation*. New York: Viking, 1971.

Oakeshott, Michael. *Experience and Its Modes*. Cambridge: Cambridge University, 1933.

Ornstein, Robert E., ed. *The Nature of Human Consciousness*. San Francisco: Freeman, 1968.

Paoli, Arturo. *Meditations on Saint Luke*. Translated by Bernard F. McWilliams. Maryknoll, N.Y.: Orbis, 1977.

Polanyi, Michael. *The Study of Man*. Chicago: University of Chicago, 1963.

Teresa, Saint. *The Complete Works of St. Teresa of Jesus.* Translated by E. Allison Peers. London: Sheed and Ward, 1946.
Trout, Kilgore. *Venus on the Half-Shell.* New York: Dell, 1974.
Uttal, William R. *The Psychobiology of Mind.* Hillsdale, N.J.: Lawrence Erlbaum Associates, 1978.
Willett, Robert F. *Primer for Christian Meditation.* Wilton, Conn.: Morehouse-Barlow, 1976.

For further study

Goleman, Daniel. *The Varieties of the Meditative Experience.* New York: Dutton, 1977.
Goleman, Daniel, and Richard J. Davidson, eds. *Consciousness: The Brain, States of Awareness, and Alternate Realities.* New York: Irvington, 1979.
James, William. *The Varieties of Religious Experience.* London: Longmans, Green, 1914.
Jaynes, Julian. *The Origin of Consciousness in the Breakdown of the Bicameral Mind.* Boston: Houghton Mifflin, 1977.
Johnston, William. *Silent Music: The Science Of Meditation.* New York: Harper and Row, 1974.
Katz, Steven T., ed. *Mysticism and Religious Traditions.* Oxford and New York: Oxford University, 1983.
Kelsey, Morton T. *The Other Side of Silence: A Guide to Christian Meditation.* New York: Paulist, 1976.
Lasch, Christopher. *The Culture of Narcissism.* New York: Norton, 1978.
Shapiro, Deane H., Jr. *Precision Nirvana: Care and Maintenance of the Mind.* Englewood Cliffs, N.J.: Prentice-Hall, 1978.
Shapiro, Deane H., Jr., and Roger N. Walsh. *The Art and Science of Meditation.* Hawthorne, N.Y.: Aldine, 1983.
Tart, Charles T. *States of Consciousness.* New York: Dutton, 1975.
Walsh, Roger N., and Frances Vaughn, eds. *Beyond Ego: Transpersonal Dimensions in Psychology.* Los Angeles: J. P. Tarcher, 1980.
White, John, ed. *What Is Meditation?* Garden City, N.Y.: Doubleday, 1974.
Zinberg, Norman E., ed. *Alternate States of Consciousness.* New York: Free Press, 1977.

Index